Elsa Tudor de Pierrefeu

"The Unity" we all need

UNITY IN THE SPIRIT

UNITY IN THE SPIRIT

By

ELSA TUDOR de PIERREFEU

RICHARD R. SMITH PUBLISHER, INC.

Rindge, New Hampshire

1955

Set up, printed and bound in the
United States of America by
The Colonial Press Inc.

TO

those great souls, children of
the Almighty Spirit, who
have come to earth to teach
us to love one another as we
would wish to be loved, for
of such is the kingdom of
heaven.

CONTENTS

CHAPTER 1

HOW IT STARTED

THIS BOOK is an outline of the object of a self-imposed mission.

St. Paul

Endeavoring to keep the unity of the Spirit in the bond of peace. Ephesians 4:3.

John Fox, Quaker

I was commanded to turn people to that inward light, Spirit and Grace, by which all might know salvation, and their way to God; even that Driving Spirit which would lead them into all Truth.

Isaiah

Arise, shine; for thy light is come, and the glory of the Lord is risen upon thee. Isaiah 60:1.

Know ye not ye are the temple of God, and that the Spirit of God dwelleth in you? 1 Corinthians 3:16.

Baha'u'llah

I have breathed in thee my Spirit, that thou mayest be my lover. Why hast thou forsaken Me and sought a beloved other than Me?

Oh Son of Being! With the hands of power I made thee and with the fingers of might I created thee, and in thee

7

have I placed the essence of my Light. Be thou content with it and see naught else, for my work is perfect and my commandment is binding. Question it not and have thou no doubt.

Similar quotations can be found in all the great religions, for Truth is one.

Since 1925 I have been interested in the release of spiritual power through world prayer by all religions in concert, not only because of the meeting of heaven and earth but to keep the Unity of the Spirit in the bond of peace.

The basic spiritual unity of mankind lies in the eternal law of the Fatherhood of God and the brotherhood of man, proclaimed by the prophets of all the great religions in the two great commandments. Mankind has fought fiercely over his diversities, not recognizing that the Almighty Spirit created diversity for very joy: joy in diversity and joy in unity.

Thou shalt love the Lord thy God with all thy heart, and with all thy soul, and with all thy mind. And. . . . thou shalt love thy neighbour as thyself.

On these two commandments hang all the law and the prophets.

Since these two commandments are indeed the basis of all the great religions, mankind actually has but one religion.

THE ONE SUPREME GOD

Buddhism—

The whole length and breadth of the wide world is pervaded by the radiant thoughts of a mind all-embracing, vast and boundless, in which dwells no hate nor ill-will.

Christianity—

There is but One God, the Father, of Whom are all things, and we are in Him.

8

Confucianism—

All things originate in and from heaven.

Hinduism—

He is the Creator, He the disposer. He Himself is one, single, one only.

Islam—

He is the First and the Last, the Seen and the Hidden.

Judaism—

The earth shall be full of the knowledge of the Lord, as the waters cover the sea.

Sikkhism—

O Lord, Thou art One, but many are Thy manifestations.

Taoism—

There is a Being wondrous and complete. Before heaven and earth It was. How calm It is! how spiritual!

Zoroastrianism—

I attribute all things to the wise Lord, the Good, Righteous, Holy, Resplendent, Glorious; to Whom belong all good things, the world, righteousness prevailing in the world, with Whose light all brilliant objects and the luminous globes are covered.

THE GOLDEN RULE

Buddhism—

Hurt not others by that which pains thyself.

Christianity—

Thou shalt love thy neighbor as thyself.

Confucianism—

What you do not like when done to thyself, do not do to others.

Hinduism—

This is the sum of duty; do naught to others which if done to thee would cause thee pain.

Islam—

No one of you is a believer until he loves for his brother what he loves for himself.

Jainism—

A man should wander about treating all creatures as he himself would be treated.

Judaism—

What thou thyself hatest do to no man.

Sikkhism—

As thou deemest thyself so deem others. Then shalt thou become a partner in heaven.

Taoism—

Rejoice at the success of others. And sympathize with their reverses, even as though you were in their place.

Zoroastrianism—

That nature only is good when it shall not do unto another whatever is not good for its own self.

It was in 1949 that this leaflet was broadcast to the world by the United Nations, the Voice of America, and WRUL. It took ten months to convince the United Nations that these two commandments were not controversial, since all believed in them except the atheists.

The inception of this work for unity in diversity really began in 1925, when I was resting and dreaming and praying on a hillside in New Hampshire, how to unite mankind in the years to come, which I foresaw would be increasingly filled with wars. The key came to me on that peaceful, sunny day amongst our New Hampshire hills. We must learn to pray together as the Christ had told us to "pray always." "Watch ye therefore, and pray always, that ye may be accounted worthy to escape all these things that shall come to pass, and to stand before the Son of man." And I remembered the daily noon prayer in Washington, D.C., during 1917 and 1918:

TO THE ALMIGHTY SPIRIT

In the year 1918 in the city of Washington, when the world was torn by the agony of the Great War, someone believed that the power of prayer would end the war. How this belief permeated and took form is not known, but the sirens blew and the church bells rang to call the people to silent prayer at noon, and the men who directed the war— men who sat up late into the night because there was never time enough for all they had to do to help their Allies in the bloody battle fields across the sea—these men stopped at noon for two minutes to pray, believing in prayer, believing in the power of united thought.

And men and women of the city stopped with them; that busy, hurried city became quiet, silent, filled with Peace.

There are those who cannot forget the beauty and power of that united thought for Peace.

These believe that men need not wait for the bloody agony to use that creative imagination which is the divine gift to every human soul. Therefore do they remind us that you and I, Beloved, wherever we are, whatever we do, may join, as

11

then, in a silent daily noon prayer for that united spirit of mankind which knows no divisions of nation or faith, but is free and full of the joy of fellowship.

Many are there who have heard the message, and all around the world they are creating by the power of their thought that unity which we all in our souls desire.

When the noon hour strikes in successive countries as the world turns toward the sun, our united thought becomes an ever-flowing river of music, harmonizing the souls of men.

O, Almighty Spirit! Fill our hearts with eternal love and Peace!

Washington, D. C.
December 9, 1926.

It was at the Boston Symphony that the invocation was given me, an invocation that anyone who believed in God could use, for this was not for Christians alone but for mankind in its hours of darkness.

This work for world peace began as early as 1916—during World War I. My husband, Alain Dedons de Pierrefeu, who was in the Battle of the Marne and then fought near Arras in the north, was injured by a "marmite" or bomb that exploded very near him and his men, with the result that the flying earth affected his eyes; and after being sent from hospital to hospital he at last was told that his damaged eyesight made him useless as a soldier. He threatened to join the Foreign Legion, but I told him he could not do that with four young children.

A few months later a family friend—an aunt of the then Secretary of State, Henry L. Stimson—was sending Dr. Wright to France to see if he could find out what the hospitals needed. Clemenceau, who was out of power, was accusing the government in his newspaper *l'Homme Libre* of being so unprepared for war that the soldiers were sleeping on the cold ground with no blankets, that there was not enough ether, not enough bandages or instruments. This was all true. The government retaliated by sending word to all hospitals that if they were asked if they needed anything they were to say they had everything. This order came to the hospital at Dinard where I was nursing, and we shrugged our shoulders. Various American organizations wanted to know what to supply, but were met with, "We have everything, thank you." When Dr. Wright came to France to find out if possible what the French wounded needed, he hired my husband to help him. At that time we were living with my husband's wealthy sister; but the only money we had was $1,000 a year left me by my aunt Mary H. Whitwell, and another $2,000 paid by my mother and two sisters to keep me from helping to support my family as a dancer on the stage. We used this money to feed our children in America, and pay for a nurse. They lived in an empty house lent us by Mr. L. B. Thatcher, my sister Delia's husband, two and a half miles out of the village of Hancock.

My husband's income had stopped when he left his job as metallurgical engineer with the Illinois Steel Company in Chicago; so he was glad to have a paid job, though he was not paid much for being an interpreter for Dr. Wright.

But within a week after Dr. Wright arrived in Paris, my husband went to the Minister of War and said, "Monsieur le Ministre, we know our government is supplying our soldiers with all the necessities, but the Americans would like to give them the superfluities. I am interpreting for Dr. Wright, who speaks no French, and it would be most useful if you would give him a permit to visit all the hospitals in Brittany so we could find out what superfluous things the Americans could supply."

The Minister of War was glad to give Dr. Wright such a permit; for thus the government's face was saved and the opening wedge was inserted, which later made it possible to get permits for all the American organizations which were anxious to help France and to get information they needed. Dinard was to be Dr. and Mrs. Wright's headquarters. They were to have gone to the hospital in Rennes the next week; but young Slater, who drove the car given him by his mother so he might be of use in France, decided he was bored and left for Paris for a spree.

M. de Pierrefeu was very angry, since neither he nor Dr. Wright (or his wife) drove. To be held up by this irresponsible, rich young American when the older men wanted to get on with their job was infuriating. M. de Pierrefeu asked at the Dinard Club if anyone would drive Dr. and Mrs. Wright and himself to Rennes the next day. An Englishman offered to do so, but the road was slippery with rain, and when the car skidded he put on his brakes. My husband and Dr. Wright were thrown from the car, which turned on its side. The driver and Mrs. Wright were unhurt; but my husband cracked his skull, and Dr. Wright broke three ribs, which was the cause of his death a year later. M. de Pierrefeu died as soon as they tried to move him.

My husband had told me, while in a hospital at Niort for examinations of his eyes, that war was horrible, and if he lived—we had both felt he would not live—he intended to spend all his time when he was not earning his living in working for peace.

After his death I felt I must try to do what he could not now do. I saw the Minister of War and asked him for a permit for the southwest part of France from Poictiers to Bordeaux, since the "Distribution Americaine," organized by Robert Bacon, then ex-Ambassador to France, would be very grateful for any help in that district. I had not the courage to go on with the work in Brittany.

He gave it immediately; I was in widow's weeds, and my husband's death was known to him because the de Pierrefeus were connected with other ancient families of France.

I had no money except what my sister-in-law felt like giving me. My husband had asked her to look after me and our children if anything happened to him, so later she gave me $1,200 yearly; but at this time I had very little.

Mrs. George McCallum told me to ask her husband to take me on this trip, but when I did he said, "I really don't feel like going."

"If you don't take me it's going to be a very long walk for me, as I intend to go somehow."

So he took me.

Mme. Boulaire and her daughter, Christiane had worked with me in the Dinard hospital, and I induced them to chaperone me. Christiane, a handsome young creature, afterward married the automobile manufacturer, Renault.

We went to all the thirty or more hospitals between Poictiers and Bordeaux; and with our authorization from the Minister of War, we got lists of all that they needed, which was far more than the mere superfluities. The "Distribution Americaine" forwarded the articles as soon as they heard from me; and before I left France from Bordeaux to go home, I wrote the Minister of War asking him to give the "Distribution Americaine" the permit he had given me. This he did; and in time all the American organizations trying to help France were given permits. Thus through my husband's diplomacy the wounded of France were helped by my people.

It is rather well understood that those of us who have Celtic blood—Scotch, Irish, Welsh—are likely to have what is often called second sight. From my mother, Elizabeth Whitwell, I have Scotch and Saxon and French blood; from my father, William Tudor, I have Scotch and Welsh. Even in childhood I sensed more than my brothers and sisters did. At six years I strongly disliked a man my father and mother had taken in to their apartment in Paris because of a hard luck story. He stayed and stayed till my mother told him he must go. I disliked him intensely, and was scolded for it. Later my parents found they had been hiding an international forger.

Prophetic dreams have come to me since I was sixteen, and oftener as I grew older.

What is real? I was dining some years ago with two old Boston friends, Isabel and Frank Grinnell, and Isabel was speaking of her interest in psychic phenomena. "I don't really believe in anything I can't touch, taste, smell or see."

"Why, Isabel," said her brilliant lawyer husband, "you can't touch, taste, smell or see any of the realities like love, truth, devotion, courage."

We are now told that even what the materialist accepts as real is an illusion of our senses, and mind, with all matter, is basically light waves; and man, too, is built of rhythmic waves of light differentiated by their speed to form the keynote, the music, of our being. "Let your light so shine before men that they may see your good works and glorify your Father which is in heaven.

In Bermuda in 1936, where I had gone to recover from the nervous strain of a divorce from a most unhappy second marriage, I had an experience that changed my plans for the future.

I had recovered my health in the lotus land of Bermuda, and had gone to the Anglican Church for the Easter service. The Scotch minister, James Watt Purves, from Edinburgh, spoke on sacrifice; and as I listened, I heard the "still, small voice" saying, "Your work is not done. You must go out into the world again."

I protested, "But I don't want to. I've done enough public work all these years since Alain died. I'm going home to New Hampshire to live quietly near my three daughters. I have more poetry to write, short stories."

"Your work for the world must go on."

"I don't want to go on. I'm tired of public work. I deserve a rest after all this unhappiness."

"You must go on."

The tears were running down my cheeks, and I gave in since I must. And then, I saw our Lord, the Christ, standing at my right hand. He was in white, but I could not see His face. On my left hand stood my dear husband, Alain.

I went to see the minister, Dr. Purves, and told him of my vision. He was very happy that it had happened in his church.

"What must you do?"

"I don't know. Perhaps I should go on with my seven years of work, from 1925 to 1932, on the noon prayer for peace."

Dr. Purves gave me a letter to the head of the Scotch Church in Edinburgh.

The next day I left by ship for New York with a friend, Stella Webber. When I woke at seven the next morning in our stateroom, I knew what I had to do. I jumped up and began dancing, saying, "Now I know what I must do! I must organize a world tour for young men to study and discuss together in the capitals of the world the problems of our time."

"How do you know?"

"I can't tell you how I know, but I woke up with this clear in my mind."

In New York I began at once seeing influential people who could help me obey the command that had been given me. And presently an executive committee and an advisory committee of important persons were formed.

Many with whom I talked feared war, and thought it too late to attempt any international project; but others believed we should work and build for peace, as the best way of preventing war.

One morning on Fifth Avenue, soon after I had talked with several key people about this project for a World Youth Tour, I saw again our Lord—this time face to face, surrounded by brilliant light. His hair was brown; His eyes dark blue; His face full of power and love and peace, with a smile in the eyes. Almost at once the vision vanished; but it convinced me that I was doing the work He wished me to do. Without His help I feel sure that the idea of World Youth discussions would never have permeated to Ministers of State; nor could I have had the perseverance and courage to organize during a time of war the Tour to South America. My confidence that this was work that our Lord wished done gave me the words and the appeal to win the co-operation of leaders and diplomats wherever I went.

CHAPTER 2

HOW IT GREW

IT WAS in 1941 that my special work began for "Unity in the Spirit."

How could we expect co-operation from temporal leaders when religious leaders did not co-operate? The spirit must lead the politicians in this dark age—Kaliyug, the Hindus call it. This I said to spiritual and religious leaders, suggesting that a beginning be made by a day of fasting and prayer together, of all those who believed in God, the leaders to agree on the day and then call on their followers by press and radio to observe this day, each religion according to its own fashion. Since we are children of one Father, therefore one family, we should be able to worship together, each according to the form of his faith. There is a Hindu saying that there are as many paths to God as there are human beings in the world. The Federation of Women's Clubs believes that we can "have unity in diversity." Diverse we are, as the flowers of the field; beautiful and satisfying is diversity, but how like we are in our fundamental unity, in our search for light, for the true, the good, the beautiful.

I hoped that the Federal Council of Churches of Christ in America would undertake this work; but when I saw Dr. Henry Smith Leiper at the Federal Council office in New York (formerly Associate Secretary of the World Council of Churches), he said it would be very difficult to bring

19

about, and very expensive. The Federal Council could not undertake it, but if I believed in it I'd better break the ground myself. If I succeeded in getting the leaders to agree on a day of prayer together, the Federal Council would of course co-operate fully. This was a blow, since I had just finished the four-year job of the Youth Tour from 1936 through 1940, and I was not at all anxious to take on another big job, especially as this would be far more difficult than the tour. In fact, everyone I saw told me it was impossible, or well-nigh impossible. But I knew someone had to tackle it. "Since you believe in it, it is for you to undertake it," said Dr. Leiper. "Why don't you go and see the Rev. John LaFarge, S.J., editor of *America?* You may tell him that if the Catholic Church will set such a day of prayer the Federal Council will agree to observe the same day."

I went at once to see Father LaFarge. I had known others of that name, relatives of his. He is tall and spare, with dark hair and brown eyes; somewhat like my father's old friend, Thomas Sergeant Perry. I told him I was from Hancock, New Hampshire, an old friend of his cousin, Margaret Perry. He warmed. "How is Margaret? I haven't seen her for some years. Has she still her herd of Guernseys?"

"Yes, but I think she may give up the milk business, because of the difficulty of getting help. Father LaFarge, I am much concerned over war and the Nazi disintegration of religion. The youth of Germany who worship Hitler will be left with a void if Hitler is beaten;—their gods will have toppled. But youth everywhere is searching for the truth— truth that they can live by. But religious leaders disagree, and quarrel. If humanity is to be helped through the dark times we live in, we must have the co-operation of all religions. I have just seen Dr. Henry Smith Leiper, to try and get the religious leaders of the world to co-operate, beginning with a day of fasting and prayer together. I hoped the Federal

20

Council would take up this work, but Dr. Henry Smith Leiper told me he thought it was almost impossible to accomplish; it was too big a job for them, and would take too much money. He sent me to you with this meassage. He thinks the idea should be carried out, and the Federal Council will agree to accept any day of prayer the Pope may set."

Father LaFarge looked astounded. Then he said, "This is amazing. I have never heard of such a plan before. I shall be glad to take it up with the National Catholic Welfare Council, and I believe they will go for it; I shall also write to Rome. I shall be glad to help you in any way I can."

"Thank you. You give me hope. I shall bother you again."

And I did. I saw him some months later. He had had no answer from Rome, but he believed I should go on trying.

"What shall I do?"

"See the other religious leaders and get their consent. You must have something concrete accomplished before the Holy Father will act. For instance, suppose I go to Archbishop Spellman and tell him I thought a new church was needed in New York. He would say to me, 'Yes, this is an excellent idea. You raise the money for the church and we will have it built.' You must see the leaders of other religions about this day of fasting and prayer to initiate co-operation. If they agree, then go to the Holy Father. I think he might consent to move."

I then began to understand what a tremendous job I had undertaken. But the only way to accomplish anything is not to be frightened by all that must be done, but to consider only the next step. Each step will take you nearer to the heaven you are trying to bring to earth.

I saw Father Gillis in New York, editor of the *Catholic World*. When I told him what I had told Father LaFarge he was even more enthusiastic than Father LaFarge. "You are another Jeanne d'Arc!"

"But I'm not Jeanne d'Arc. This mission is too big for me."

"With the help of God you can go on and succeed. Keep at it every day."

"Father Gillis, if you and others help me it can be done. I shall need all the help that can be given me. Write to Rome, so that the Holy Father may know that someone is working. I cannot get to Rome during war, but letters still go."

"I will see what I can do. Pray to Jeanne d'Arc and Our Lady. They will help you."

"I prayed to Notre Dame de Lourdes when I was at Lourdes in 1937. I felt she blessed the work I was then doing. Monsieur de Pierrefeu's body and his father's are both buried at Lourdes; they were both good Catholics. Good-bye, Father."

"Good-bye, Madame."

To give an account of all those I saw in our country, or even all those in other parts of the world, would make this too long. I saw Catholics, Protestants and Jews in New York, Boston and San Francisco. I saw Indian Swamis in Boston, Washington, and San Francisco. These last of course appreciated the mission, because they have been teaching the fundamental unity of religions in America ever since Swami Vivekananda first came to America when I was a child. I remember being taken to a lecture of his at the Henry Lee Higginsons'.

In Boston I saw Dr. Kirtley F. Mather, whom I had known for some years as a thoughtful and liberal-minded man. He had helped me to get Harvard University to send a study group to South America. He was the Director of the Summer School in 1940. I wanted his advice and reaction to the co-operation of religious leaders for unity. He was definitely interested, and gave me the following letter of approval.

HARVARD UNIVERSITY
Department of Geology and Geography
Geological Museum

September 14, 1943

Dear Comtesse:

I am very much interested in your proposal that a "universal day of prayer" be established, on which the adherents of all the great religions of the world would join. The undertaking is obviously a most difficult one, but it certainly will never be accomplished unless an attempt is made to realize it. It would be much more than a mere gesture, indicative of the fundamental unity of the scattered and diversified forces of religion. Its repercussions for good might well surprise even you and me.

I would suppose that Protestants, Catholics, Jews, Mohammedans, Buddhists, and all the other faiths could unite in a common petition for forgiveness of sins and for a strengthening of the spiritual forces in the universe. Perhaps the theologians can indicate other uniformities that they have discovered in their study of comparative theology.

If I can be of any assistance to you in accomplishing this object, please feel free to call upon me.

Cordially yours,
Kirtley F. Mather

He advised me to see Dean Willard Sperry of the Harvard Divinity School on Francis Street, near the University, and I went at once from his office. Mrs. Sperry answered the bell, and told me her husband had broken his wrist, but she would see if he felt like seeing me. While she went to him, I prayed that he would see me. She came back and asked me to go up to her husband's study. There I found him, a fine-looking man, easy to talk to. I told him about the day of fasting and prayer and the need for unity, and he advised me not to form a committee.

"Don't start an organization, but just go and see the leaders and try to get their consent."

"I agree with you, Dean Sperry; there are too many organizations already, and they slow up the work."

"I shall be glad to help you if I can. I doubt if I can be of any use with President Roosevelt, to get your permission to travel abroad, but perhaps a letter would help. Let me know when and how I can help you. I am all in favor of unity in the spirit, and more co-operation, but it's difficult to bring the Protestants and Catholics together. We have tried but with little success."

"Thank you; you have given me hope and courage."

This was Dean Sperry's letter:

HARVARD DIVINITY SCHOOL

September 21, 1943

Dear Countess de Pierrefeu:

Please forgive my delay in sending you this promised letter. As you saw, I was—and still am—housed, and have to get on with my correspondence slowly.

You laid before me your hope that, somehow or other, a world-wide day of fasting and prayer might be arranged in which all religious folk of good will might feel united in what would be a common act of penitence and self-dedication.

No one who cares for religion can for a moment question the desirability of such a day and such an act, and many individuals and religious bodies would be glad to be identified with such an act and associated together in its observance. The principle is simple and clear; there remains the matter of practice.

As you well enough know, no single individual or small

24

group of individuals can hope to promote the organization necessary for the effective observance of such a day. It would have to be done through existing religious bodies.

If it is done, it should be done freely and *con amore*, as a co-operative act, so that each participating body recognizes to the full the right of others to share in the act. If I were you I should stress this latter point in whatever further approaches you make.

With best wishes,
Sincerely yours,
W. H. Sperry

I saw Bishop Henry K. Sherrill, whom I knew slightly. He was at the Diocesan House in Boston, but very busy at the time, and spoke to me only for a few moments, without even sitting down. I did not feel I had made any impression on him, but in later years he more than made up for this hurried reception. He must have thought, "Another dreamer who thinks she has the solution." But when I stuck to the work in later years he must have changed his mind.

I wrote to Dr. Temple, Archbishop of York, and received the following answer. This letter, as will be seen later, was important.

Bishopthorpe,
York   April 12, 1941
Dear Madame,

As a sign of unity in the spirit, I should welcome the plan you describe, but I am not sufficiently interested in it to take any initiative amid the vast multitude of concerns with which I am attempting to deal.

Yours very truly,
William Ebor

I wrote to Gandhi who was a political prisoner in the Aga Khan's palace, and in time received the following postcard:

Dear Sister,

I would gladly co-operate. But in the midst of hypocrisy I doubt the utility of composite public fast. Fasting and prayer of the type you have in mind should be in secret and with a definite object.

Yours sincerely,
M. K. Gandhi

His experiences justified his accusation of hypocrisy. He had seen only too much of it in his dealings with the British Lion. But neither Gandhi's discouraging card nor any other discouragement kept me from going on. What seemed impossible to men was not impossible to God, and I worked for God.

In 1941 and 1942 I was in San Francisco. I saw Bishop Karl M. Block of the Episcopal Church, and I showed him some of my letters. He seemed troubled by Gandhi's postcard. "Are we hypocrites?"

"Sometimes we are—often politically. We pretend we are honest and aboveboard, but consider our histories and the detours we have made to get what we want," I answered.

"I was thinking more of the churches. My experience with our Protestant churches has been one of frankness, on the whole."

All I accomplished with Bishop Block was that he knew of the work. Usually it was a case of casting the idea upon the soil and hoping it had fallen onto good earth where it could grow.

In Washington, D. C., I saw Monsignor John A. Ryan, whom I had met through Justice Louis D. Brandeis. I had known Justice and Mrs. Brandeis since I was twelve years old, through Elizabeth Glendower Evans. She and the Brandeises lived on Otis Place in Boston, just around the corner from 37 Brimmer Street, where my grandfather, William

Scollay Whitwell, had given us a home with him because my father had had financial losses. Brave Elizabeth Evans picketed during strikes, and helped Sacco and Vanzetti in their seven-year struggle for life; she was always on the side of the helpless and downtrodden. When I decided to picket munition factories in 1931, I went to her for advice on how to do it. I had become a friend of the Brandeises through the years, and always saw them when I was in Washington. The Justice was a great soul; our Secretary of State, Dean Acheson, was fortunate to have been his secretary for two years, and America was fortunate that this was so. Justice Brandeis said to me when John G. Winant was Governor of New Hampshire, "John Winant is an unusual man. Look into his eyes and truth shines there."

I told Monsignor Ryan my hope of getting the leaders of religion to co-operate, and asked him if he would help me.

"What can I do?"

"I want your moral support, and I want to reach not only religious leaders but the Presidents of the A. F. of L. and the C. I. O."

"I can give you introductions to William Green and Philip Murray and Cordell Hull."

I knew Cordell Hull, but was grateful to get introductions to Green and Murray. Green I was never able to see—in spite of (or perhaps because of) his having been a clergyman; he did not even honor Monsignor Ryan's letter. Green's secretary was much interested in my work, but telephoned me she could not get me an appointment to see Green. I tried Murray, and was given an appointment but when I went, Murray's secretary told me he had been called in to see President Roosevelt and could not, of course, keep his appointment with me. His secretary advised me to try and see him in Philadelphia, as the annual meeting of the C.I.O. delegates was being held there the next day. I should be able to see Murray there.

I went to the Bellevue Stratford in Philadelphia the next day, and found it full of labor leaders. I did not know how to get to Murray, and asked two very tall young negroes. They were snooty to a degree that surprised me, since I had been very polite. "Ask someone else!" So I did, and was told to find the Executive Secretary in a room to the left of the stage of the large auditorium. Such a friendly man! I showed him my letter from Monsignor Ryan. "President Murray is going to make a speech, but if you'll wait you can see him as he comes out."

"Can't I sit in the hall so as to hear President Murray?"

"Come with me and you can hear him."

I followed him up some steps, and before I knew what was happening I was seated on the stage not far from President Murray and Sidney Hillman. I chuckled to myself. What would my conservative Boston friends think of me sitting on the platform at a C.I.O. meeting?

Soon after I was seated, Sidney Hillman began addressing the delegates. He made an impassioned plea for them to vote for Roosevelt (F.D.R.) as a friend of labor. When he sat down, President Murray got up and made his address, not impassioned, but quietly spoken. He advised the delegates not to pledge themselves to Roosevelt, until they knew what Roosevelt would do for labor. "Wait and see. We must keep the President guessing as to whom we will vote for."

But the speeches were more particularly on the forming of a political action committee, the beginning of a real labor party.

When Murray had done I went up to him and asked if I could speak to him. He was hurrying down to talk and meet with the delegates.

"I'm afraid I haven't the time now, but ask my secretary to make an appointment for you."

"I'm sorry, President Murray. I followed you here from Washington to try and get a few minutes with you; but this

28

I will say. Today, with this new political action committee, labor in America has come of age."

He smiled; then several other people took his attention. I never did get to talk to him, because I did not keep after him as one must in order to get results.

Outside of Philadelphia, at Haverford College, I saw Friend Rufus Jones. He did not remember my appealing to him in 1925 for a daily noon prayer for peace, but I remembered him.

He was no longer very active, though I last saw and heard him speak in New York City for freedom for India; what he said was wise, logical, and full of common sense.

Now as I told him of the great need of unity in the spirit among religions, he agreed with Dean Sperry that it was better not to organize the work with committees and sponsors. "But what can I do to help?"

"Would you help me to get to Europe, the Middle East, and India? I cannot induce the State Department to give me visas or in fact get abroad at all."

"I doubt if you will be allowed to travel while we're at war, but I will see the President for you." Then he smiled.

"I can always see him, but Franklin Roosevelt has a way of conversing so continuously to keep me from asking for what I want that I usually go away without being able to speak at all, much less get what I came for."

Archbishop Athenagoras, Archbishop Cushing—all the important exponents of the faiths had to be reached. I found that the head of the Greek Orthodox Churches was in New York—Archbishop Athenagoras of North and South America. I made no appointment—just rang the bell of the big house on 70th Street and asked to see the Archbishop. I first inquired how to address him, and was told, "His Excellency." I was in a large hall more like a large room. The house had formerly been a private dwelling. There were two desks, with two priests working, and I asked one if I could see the Archbishop. I gave my card. (The main reason I use my husband's title is because of my work. It means something to Europeans and diplomats.) The priest took it upstairs, and came down with the message that His Excellency would see me in fifteen minutes. I waited and prayed. He took me into a further small parlor or waiting room, lighted by electricity. I sat and prayed. It was not more than fifteen minutes before the same secretary came back, and showed me upstairs through a large handsome parlor into a study. There behind a table was the Archbishop—a very tall, handsome, distinguished personage, with large dark eyes and black hair and beard. He asked me to be seated near his big desk and tell him what I wanted. I then explained why I had come to him and what I was attempting to do. He was most attentive.

"Your Excellency, I am trying to get visas so I can see the Patriarch in Istanbul, but so far have not been able to get permission to travel because of the war."

"I feel sure this is a feasible mission, but a very difficult one. His Holiness, the Patriarch, will be deeply interested. He will certainly wish to co-operate. There is no doubt that those who believe in God should be able to work together and pray together, but so far it is not being done. What can I do for you?"

"Will you give me a letter saying what you think of this effort? That would be a help."

"Certainly I will, as I think highly of your endeavor. I pray it may be successful."

I was impressed with this man's devotion and spirituality to such a degree that I asked him to give me his blessing. I have been blessed by Catholic Cardinals and by Dr. Davidson, Archbishop of Canterbury; and I know I was strengthened. Archbishop Athenagoras came from behind his desk. I took off my hat and knelt. He laid his hands on my head and blessed me. I rose and thanked him.

"I shall pray for your success."

"I shall need your prayers. Thank you, Your Excellency."

I waited a year for an appointment with Archbishop Richard J. Cushing of Boston—his many new duties kept him much tied up. I did see the Archbishop's secretary, Monsignor John J. Wright (now Bishop Wright), in Worcester, Massachusetts, in 1941, and explained to him why I wanted to see the Archbishop.

Monsignor Wright was slender and handsome, with dark hair and eyes. He has a brilliant mind and should go far. He knew Rome well, since he had studied there. I gave him Father LaFarge's reaction to the work of Unity, as well as that of several other prominent men. He must have been impressed by my zeal, as Father Lord had been, for he too hinted that I might succeed sooner as a Catholic.

"Monsignor, I nearly became a Catholic when I was first married. I went to Bishop Whitehead in Newark, New Jersey. He asked me if I wanted with all my heart and soul to be a Catholic.

" 'No, I only thought it would be happier for my husband and children.' "

" 'That is not enough; you must long for it wholeheartedly.' "

"So I did not become a Catholic. I can be of much more use to my husband's Church out of it than in it. If I speak well of it, it will mean far more than my doing so as a Catholic."

Then I made the following remark, because I recognized that Monsignor Wright had the good of the Catholic Church at heart.

"Monsignor, the great weakness of the Catholic Church is its desire for temporal power. Père de la Chapelle, a cousin

31

of my husband's, who married us, told me in 1926 that what the Church needed was martyrs to strengthen her. She is having martyrs now under Hitler."

"It is true, Madame, that our Church has her weakness, but she is being strengthened."

He rose in my estimation, for it is rare to acknowledge a weakness in the love of one's life.

At last I was to see the Archbishop, and I went as usual with prayers in my heart that he might give me help. I did not have to wait very long for His Excellency at the Archbishopric. He greeted me kindly, and I kissed his amethyst ring. He gave me the feeling that he could give me all the time I wanted. This is rare in prominent men, who are apt to be so filled with their own importance that they make you feel that you must hurry.

I was with the Archbishop for nearly an hour; he seemed to want to hear all that I hoped to accomplish. He not only listened, but asked questions; but he gave no opinion.

"Your Excellency, your Church is highly organized. It has power. It could do much in bringing together the other religious leaders for prayer, for the peace of the world."

"It is not easy to convince other religious leaders that they should work with us."

"I know, but the effort must be made. The Catholic Church has long known the danger of Godless communism. We are all in danger, and must stand together."

"This is true, and the Holy Father has called on other faiths to pray with the Catholics."

"Yes, I know; but it is not only prayer but co-operative action that is needed. If those who believe in God cannot stand together, the religions would be destroyed from within, one after another; and without faith the human race is lost."

I gave him the names and opinions of some of the men I had seen.

32

"What are you intending to do next?"

"I want visas for England, France, Egypt, and India. In Cairo I want to see the religious leader of the Mohammedans. The Egyptian Ambassador told me to see the President of Al Azhar University. I want to see the Holy Father in Rome."

"How can I help you?"

"Will you write to President Roosevelt and ask him to help me get my passports and visas? Though we are at war I should be seeing the religious leaders."

"I will."

I was astonished and delighted that he would help me. I thanked him heartily, and kissing his ring made my adieux.

When I had seen the top men and many others of importance in America, I began in 1943 to try to get to Egypt and India in spite of war. As I needed a British visa, I wrote to Sir Stafford Cripps, in the British Cabinet, and to Lord Temple, in the House of Lords (now Archbishop of Canterbury), to ask them to intercede to allow me to get to the Middle East and India. I wrote to both the same day, and received their answers on the same day. Sir Stafford said he was sorry not to be able to help me, but it was against the Government policy, "and I think you will understand." I did, of course. Archbishop Temple wrote the following:

Lambeth Palace, S.E.I.,
Dec. 9, 1943

Dear Madam,

I am afraid I do not now remember what passed between us in 1941 when I was at York, but I have never consciously commended a plan for combining all religions in any enterprise. As a rule I think that kind of effort entirely misplaced, because the distinction between Christianity and the other

33

religions cuts so deep. I think it therefore most unlikely that I should find myself able to support the plan which you now describe to me.

Yours faithfully,
William Cantuar.

I wrote to Dr. Temple after receiving his second letter: "I realize that I have placed you in a very difficult position in asking you to use your influence with the Tory Government in my behalf, as the Anglican Church is a State Church and owes its allegiance first to the State, second to God, but your defection will weaken the work I am trying to do. However, I know you will want all those who are giving me their support to know how you now feel."

Bishop H. St. George Tucker was Presiding Bishop of the Protestant Episcopal Church in 1943. I had been to him, and he was enthusiastic and most kind, as this letter shows:

September 17th, 1943

My dear Comtesse,

This is just a line to assure you of my interest in your plans for a Universal Day of Prayer.

I wish that I could offer you concrete suggestions as to how this plan might best be carried out, but at the present time all that I can do is to express my willingness to co-operate. I hope that your faith in this plan will be rewarded by an opening of the way to its execution. Also I hope that you may find many who will, like myself, be glad to co-operate with you.

If it would be of any service to you, I shall be glad to have you use this letter in presenting your plan to any you may approach.

Certainly we must hold to our belief that things which ought to be done will, by God's help, finally become possible.

With kind regards, I am
Yours very sincerely,
H. St. George Tucker

He agreed to go to see President Roosevelt to urge my being allowed to get to Egypt and India; and Dr. Israel Goldstein, President of the Synagogue Council of America, had agreed to go with him.

SYNAGOGUE COUNCIL OF AMERICA

November 29, 1943

My dear Comtesse:

The Synagogue Council would be glad to go along with the Federal Council of Churches in your proposal. Likewise, I shall be pleased to join a delegation to Washington.

Your interest in the advancement of the spiritual unity deserves every encouragement. I pray that your efforts may be successful.

Sincerely yours,
Dr. Israel Goldstein
President

When, however, I informed all those who had said they believed in this work of Unity in the Spirit, that the Archbishop of Canterbury no longer believed in this work, Bishop Tucker wrote me that it would be embarrassing for him to push something that Archbishop Temple did not believe in. Monsignor Ryan had written me to the same purpose. I was more taken aback by my own Bishop than by the Catholic John Ryan, since I had such enthusiasm for him. I was again shocked, as I had been by the Archbishop of Canterbury's change of mind; but this time to realize how closely our Protestant Church, which is supposed to be free, was affected by the Anglican Church, a State Church. Again I do not criticize another's action, for I am not in his position. If I were, I might do the same; and I know what a fine man Bishop Tucker is.

The Archbishop's change of mind about Unity in the Spirit was a shock, and at first I could find no excuse for him, but as I considered the fact that the Anglican Church is a State Church and therefore must follow the State's policies, I could see how difficult it would have been for Dr. Temple to interfere in my behalf to carry on the effort for Unity in the Spirit in India, since the State worked to divide the Hindus and Mohammedans so as to rule India. Winston Churchill had publicly said that the financial state of India affected the lives of one man out of nine in the British Isles, and he had no intention of giving up India.

The following leaders had given me their letters of approval and in most cases had offered their co-operation:

Archbishop Athenagoras, head of the Greek Orthodox Church of North and South America.

Bishop H. St. John Tucker, Presiding Bishop of the Episcopal Church in America and President of the Federal Council of the Churches of Christ in America.

Dr. Samuel McCrea Cavert, General Secretary of the Federal Council of Churches of Christ in America.

Father John LaFarge, Editor of *America*.

Monsignor John A. Ryan.

Dr. Israel Goldstein, President of the Jewish Synagogues of North America.

Lord Lang, Archbishop of Canterbury in 1941.

Rufus Jones, and the American Friends Service Committee.

The President and Staff of The National Conference of Christians and Jews.

Dr. Emory Ross, General Secretary of the Foreign Missions of North America.

Dr. T. L. Yuan, Director of Peiping University.

Mahatma Gandhi would be glad to co-operate, but felt that there was too much hypocrisy in the world today.

Dean Willard L. Sperry of the Harvard Divinity School.

Dr. Mary E. Woolley.

Rev. E. Stanley Jones.

Rt. Rev. Carl Block, Bishop of California.
Swami Premananda.

Bishop H. St. John Tucker (Bishop Tucker writes that the
Archbishop of Canterbury might change his mind in time.
"We know that great men are not afraid to change their
minds." (But within the year Dr. Temple was dead.)

Many have remained silent.

At this time I saw Dean Sperry about Dr. Temple's decision. I said I had had a letter from the Archbishop saying he
had changed his mind about the work for co-operation
among the religious leaders. Dean Sperry said, "He is a great
friend of mine, but a very busy man. I, who know him well,
would not ask him to write even a few words of introduction
to the book I am working on, so you should not expect his
help."

"But this is not a question of time, Dean Sperry, but of a
retraction. Read these two letters."

He did so.

"Well, of course I can't agree that the distinction between
Christianity and the other religions cuts so deep."

Then later I saw Rufus Jones in his study at Haverford
College, and I said I would like to show him two letters from
Dr. Temple.

"He is a great friend of mine." I handed him the letters.
All he said was,

"This is very sad," and he looked sad, and handed them
back to me.

Later he wrote me that he did not see how I could go on
without Dr. Temple's support. I answered that Unity of
Spirit among men was the teaching of all the really great
teachers, and I could not give up the work because one man

of importance no longer believed in it. I said I was sure it was not my work, but God's.

Here is his answer:

RUFUS M. JONES
Haverford College
Haverford, Pa.
4-5-1944

My dear friend,

Many thanks for your interesting letter of March 31st.

I agree fully with you that under the circumstances it is right to go ahead with your plan, and I shall be quite ready to give whatever backing to it I can.

I was very glad to hear that you had been at the Friends Meeting in Cambridge. It is a beautiful Meeting and one of the very best in New England.

With warm regards,
Sincerely your friend,
Rufus M. Jones

Rufus Jones was a great Quaker, but he would have been a great soul whatever his religion. These are some of his beliefs:

"The man who has yielded to temptation and finally won his spiritual battle, is a stronger man than the one who has never known sin."

"The world within is as real as the world without."

"Love works and works triumphantly, at the heart of things."

How to get to Egypt and India? One day I saw four or five lines in the *Boston Globe* on an inside page that Under Secretary of State Dean Acheson had studied law at Harvard as a student of Felix Frankfurter (now Justice Frankfurter), and that they were good friends. I had known the Justice for twenty years, and I had talked with him in 1941 in his office at the Supreme Court, about the need for unity in the religious world. As I left him he had said, "As Justice I cannot take any part in world affairs, but certainly there is nothing more important than unity among men today." So now I wrote him to say I needed to get to Europe, Egypt, and India to go on with my work; could he say a good word for me to Dean Acheson? The Justice did not answer, but four days later I received a letter from the Under Secretary of State in which he said that Justice Frankfurter had spoken to him of my work, and if I came to Washington he would like to talk to me about it.

I sped to Washington, and as soon as I telephoned I was given an appointment for the next day. I told Dean Acheson what I was doing, and named some of the people who were standing by me. I suggested the importance to the world of the co-operation of all those who believed in God—that the world must stand and work together as the atheist Communist world was doing. I must get to Europe and India to reach the leaders of other religions; and I needed help. I might be able to reach the youth of these countries too.

Dean Acheson asked me what help I needed.

"I need a passport and visas. I need a letter from you to all our diplomatic officers, like the one Cordell Hull gave me in 1936 when I was organizing the World Youth Tour."

"We cannot give such letters, as they were misused during the war; but I will notify our diplomatic officers to give you your passport and what help they can, if you will keep me informed of where you are going." He was as good as his word. Without his help the interviews would have taken very long to get. I wish to thank our former Secretary of State who had a vision of what this work could do to unite theists for the good of our world, which is in such danger now.

I am now overcome with my own blindness to the facts of Empire; but is not this very fact of the desire for power over one's fellow men the avowed reason for fighting Hitler and the Japanese? Have we not got to face what is evil in Hitler and the military caste in Japan as equally evil for the United Nations? It is not easy to face the evil in our own hearts. Any one of us may be faced in our public or private life with as difficult a decision as was that of the Archbishop's. Are we sure we should choose the road of the Spirit rather than the illusion of an easier road to a temporal and worldly end? The essence of the great war of today is that choice of the individual between the highest allegiance he knows and temporal expedience. The temptations are insidious, and the best of us may fail.

We do not agree with the Archbishop that this sort of effort is entirely misplaced because the distinction between Christianity and the other religions cuts so deep. We know that comparative religion has taught and yielded to Christian teaching and belief the best in the five outstanding religions of the world, which we have taken over and wrought into the fabric of Christian idealism, making Christian theology and doctrine richer in its quality, giving strength to its appeal and eternal worth. The Hindus accept all the religions as facets of the diamond of truth. A Swami in Washington has above him as he preaches, an oil painting of our Lord the Christ in His spiritual agony on the Mount of Olives. The Koran says, "We believe in God and that which hath been done unto Abraham, and Ishmael, and Isaac, and Jacob, and the Tribes, and that which was delivered unto Moses, and Jesus, and that which was delivered unto the prophets from the Lord: We make no distinction between any of them and to God are we resigned."

Are the followers of these religions so much kinder and more embracing to the teachers and prophets sent by God to men than are the Christians? Can anyone believe it is the will of our loving Lord the Christ that those who profess to follow Him should allow that the distinction between His teaching and that of other great teachers cuts so deep we cannot combine all religions in any enterprise, not even to pray to our One Father together? God forbid! The tide of life, love, sympathy, and brotherhood cannot be damned in its upward sweep by any such breakwaters of the past.

Many German Catholic priests and Lutheran pastors have gone to prison and death rather than put their allegiance to God second to their allegiance to the State. Have we less courage?

CHAPTER 3

TO ENGLAND

IF YOU haven't traveled on a luxury liner re-conditioned as a troop ship you don't know how our boys traveled, packed nearly as tight as sardines—not only in the staterooms but in the dining room, the library, and the once spacious lounges. There were five women in our cabin on Deck A, but three tiers of iron berths, with three berths on each tier.

A six-foot New Hampshire sergeant, coming home from the Pacific, said of his berth, "I couldn't sit up in it; I crouched." I too crouched in mine on the *Argentina,* and I'm not six feet. If you were too ancient to climb into the second or third berth, you sat on the edge of the lowest and rolled in; but if you were in the second, as I was, you grabbed the iron that ran from top to bottom of the three berths, then stepped on the lower berth (not on its occupant), threw your left leg onto the rail of the top berth, with your right arm at the same time grasping your own berth, hoisted with your left arm, swung up your right leg, got both knees on your berth, bent double, and wondered how you were going to wriggle into a lengthwise position, since the top berth was so low that you were afraid of catching your hair in its springs, or rolling back onto the floor from four feet up. Somehow I didn't roll out. When at last I was straightened out on my berth, with my arms close against its iron sides, I was not the princess who could feel a pea beneath six featherbeds, because my mattress was just about two inches thick; though neither of hair nor feathers; anyway, I slept.

We were all in bed, the little white-haired Scotch lady beneath me, the heavy Yorkshire grandmother across the way, over her an English-born American, and below across the portholes a young American whose husband, on the lowest rung of the diplomatic service, was sleeping next door with some men.

"Ladies, aren't you thankful you don't have to share your berth with a husband?" I asked. They chuckled.

"Let him try it."

I thought of the coffins certain monks sleep in to remind them of their demise. My berth was as narrow and nearly as hard.

There was a bathroom between our room and the room "the" husband used with three other men. The Yorkshire grandmother came to us with a red face.

"Did ye know the men next doorr make use of ourr bath and toilet? I met one as I was comin' oot—verra embarrassin'! It shouldn'a be permitted. They should use the public baths. I should speak to the purrser."

But the purser said it was none of his business.

"I canna' underrstand such goin's on. It's no rrespectable."

So I went to see the purser—one of the five or six in khaki behind the bar.

"Don't tell me you're all pursers."

"Yes."

"Which is the most important?"

"I suppose I am."

So I explained how shocked and grieved our Yorkshire grandmother was when she met a male near our bathroom or in it; and couldn't their door be locked so they couldn't get to "our" bathroom.

"I have no key, but the steward can lock it. Tell him to."

And I did; and the next we knew the four men had been

43

moved to another room and their former room closed and locked; but even so I don't think our Yorkshire lady was properly grateful.

She showed us an old-fashioned gold watch and chain.

"I am givin' my daughters in England all me jewelry because I may die on this jourrney." The tears filled her eyes. "Me husband is as strong as a bull; he would prrobably marry again; and I don't intend me jewelry to go to his second wife. Me doctorr warrned me I must be less active if I wish to live ten or twenty yearrs longerr. I left the hoos in pairrfect orrderr, mended everry last bit. Me husband said, 'There's still one thing to do before you leave; sew a button on me coat.' So I sewed it on for him."

I corralled two American Friends Service men on board going to France and Poland to distribute food by truck. Then I invited two Indian students, one from Calcutta and the other from Trinidad, to join us at table. Fate gave us a former Welsh miner and his wife. The miner told me he had worked eighteen years in the Welsh coal mines, and some months in coal mines in Pennsylvania.

"Lewis is dead right to ask first for better living conditions for the miners and greater safety. In Wales we have the eight-hour day. If a man is found even with a stump of a cigarette in his pocket he is fined two pounds. The danger from coal gas is greater in Wales than in America; but even so the American should have an electric light bulb to wear on his forehead as the Welshman does. The American has to buy his own light, and uses an open flame. There are more accidents in America—usually one a day; one reason for this is that the coal is dynamited, but in Wales picks are used. The Americans hold up the roof with wooden supports. I have seen a support as big around as a man's body shivered to splinters by the weight of the ceiling. In Wales the miners have to shovel and pack up the sides of the shaft with earth

44

that can bear the weight over their heads. I will never go down into a mine again. I don't like to think about it or talk about it. Lewis knows well what the men need and should have."

"It seems to me that occupations should be paid for according to their danger: miners, fire-fighters, airplane pilots, train engineers, seamen, should get more than men and women who do not daily risk life and limb."

"Of course they should, but they aren't."

Our gay, funny little Scot, with unending stories, who loved the fifty-nine children on our ship, made friends with the highbrows, the Negro lawyer going to college in Scotland, the businessmen, the mothers.

One night in our stateroom at eleven-thirty we had a songfest. The lady from Yorkshire, extended in her berth, the lovely looking wife of forty-six on a vacation from her husband and two grown children, our Scot and I sang heart-moving old Irish melodies, then English, then Gilbert and Sullivan; the little Scotch woman dancing and acting out the parts. She was a fairy and an angel, who mislaid her pocketbook and her sewing kit; anyway, why should angels bother with the whereabouts of pocketbooks, needles and thread, and such-like earthy things?

It took us two hours to find and collect our luggage for the customs at Southampton. A young woman from Montreal, with an eighteen-months old baby who had neither slept nor eaten properly on shipboard, seemed bewildered.

"Will the train wait for me? I have not bought a ticket. I have only two of my pieces of luggage here. How shall I get the rest?"

"The porters are bringing the luggage alphabetically. What is your name?"

"O'Neill."

45

"That's just before me. I am "P". Sit down on the luggage stand and your bags will come. Perhaps you'd better get your train ticket. Leave the baby with me."

But the baby wouldn't be left, so she went for her ticket with the child in her arms. When she came back, a kind man got her a chair, and the child promptly went to sleep on her shoulder; but she woke up in ten minutes because she was hungry. So I fished out some trisket and fed her small bits at a time; and I found some nuts for Mrs. O'Neill.

I noticed a man give one of the customs officers a bar of chocolate after inspection. The man slipped it into his inner pocket and looked so well pleased that after he had finished my luggage I offered him an orange. He at first refused, but I urged him and he took it. Oranges in England were for babies and children only.

On the train I sat opposite a young woman who had just finished her tea. I still had some nuts and was eating a few and offered her some.

"Nuts! I haven't seen any for so long. But you must not deprive yourself."

"But I want you to have some. I don't need them."

"How kind you are! Such a treat!"

She ate all I gave her, slowly and with relish. Expecting dinner on the train, I had not ordered tea; but there was no dinner, so I asked the polite waiter what he could give me for tea.

"We have ham and sardine sandwiches, Madame."

I took sardines, which are not vegetarian; but like George Arliss, I sometimes eat fish when there is nothing else.

When I got to the hotel at 10:30 I was hungry, and asked if I could get something to eat.

"We can give you sardine sandwiches, Madame."

Again I ate sardine sandwiches—and was glad to get them.

I had tea at an English friend's house the next afternoon and was telling her about my sardine debauch.

"I thought of giving you sardine sandwiches myself."

That night I was telling my room waiter about the sardines. He laughed.

"We've just had a load of sardines from Portugal, Madame; that is why there are plenty of them."

The lumps of sugar here were a third the size of ours. I was given one of these for a cup of unsweetened cocoa, which merely made it less bitter, so I called on the telephone and asked if it were possible to have two lumps. The waiter returned with two more lumps.

"We are allowed to serve two lumps for tea but only one for dinner, Madame. We are given three lumps a day for each guest."

"Can't you pretend this is tea? I don't want to be a pig, but I don't want the cocoa if it hasn't some sweetness. Take one of these lumps back and I'll have just the one cup of cocoa."

"You'd better keep it, Madame, for breakfast. Some people don't take sugar so we have a little over," and he put it in the drawer of the desk. "So there it is."

The maid was discussing the price of clothes with me.

"I did want a suit that was not utility. We get very tired of the utility clothes. They's not badly cut but the cloth is thin, not warm enough for winters. I priced a suit at Selfridge's. The cheapest was twenty pounds. I couldn't go that."

Twenty pounds would be eighty dollars. I myself wouldn't put all that into a suit if I could help it.

"This is a lovely hat, Madame. May I look at it?"

"All you want to."

I suppose I should have given it to her; but it was a three-year-old black winter hat and I hated to shop for another the next fall.

That Sunday afternoon a young London friend took me to see some of the blitzed areas. We did not see the docks, which suffered the worst destruction, but we did see "the city." As we walked by the acres of open spaces, where nothing remained but the crumbled foundations, I thought of the ruins of Karnak in Egypt, the ruins of Pompeii. Yellow flowers and grass were growing in the ground and the crannies of broken brick walls, even little trees. Archaeologists uncover layers of ancient destroyed cities, and dig to discover what people once lived in these buried and forgotten ruins. What energy, what sweat and toil, men spend on these transient buildings. Nations rise and fall, like the waves on the great ocean of life. May we of the Americas build joy as well as beauty, before the wave of our strength subsides into the bosom of life itself.

My sister-in-law, Countess Jehan de Pierrefeu, whose husband was killed in August, 1918, in a hopeless sortie, had four of our boys quartered on her before "D" Day. "Babies," she called them, though they were eighteen and twenty. "They behaved like perfect gentlemen. They were so glad to have all the baths they wanted. They came in filthy from handling the big guns, but you wouldn't believe how they cleaned up. Three of my boys were terribly afraid of being afraid. We had about 16,000 men in this town, and everybody loved them. The Americans are so friendly and so gay."

"Were there any unpleasant incidents?" I asked.

"Not one that I know of in this district. We English are slow to make friends—too reserved; but your boys have made quite a change in us. We talk to strangers now. Our boys as they march by never turn their heads or look at us, but your boys wave at us, call out 'Hi'—and smile. I was in London doing canteen work for the men who had to demolish blitzed buildings that might fall and injure people.

48

The Londoners were so exhausted that the government called for volunteers from the country for canteen work—mostly middle-aged women, since the young women were in factories or with the armed forces. I had no one dependent on me, so I volunteered (she was sixty); we were in a hotel near Victoria Station, dirty but with beds. We worked eight to nine hours taking coffee and sandwiches to the demolition men. I *was* tired that first night, but I couldn't get to sleep, there was such a racket from the street cars—such a noise! At two in the morning the janitor knocked. 'Better come down to the lounge, it's safer there; the doodle bugs have been coming pretty thick.' I put on slacks over my pajamas, snatched a coat and jersey, and went down. The other women were there. The janitor said we'd better go down into the shelter. I'm such a coward! I went. I knew I'd not be any good the next day if I got no sleep. It *was* quiet in the shelter—not a sound. I took a sleeping tablet like most of the others, and slept like a log. At the end of two weeks I went home, that's all anyone could stand. I stood in a queue for two hours at the station to get onto the train; there was such a crowd trying to get out of London. When the gates opened we made a mad rush, but I got no seat. I stood in the train, jammed in with the crowd, for four hours, until we got to Exmouth. I was *so* tired I just tumbled into bed when I got home."

An Exmouth policeman speaks.

"As you know, the public places great reliance on the police. Some of you were present when a telephone call came from a lady who asked me to stop a Nazi plane from flying over her house, as she felt sure it was going to drop a bomb. I assured her that the complaint would be attended to at once; that apparently made her happy.

"One night when bombs began to fall in the town, a War Reserve constable, who was slightly deaf in one ear, saw his colleagues dive under the desk in the Charge Room and

49

thought they had taken leave of their senses. When he realized what was happening, the whole of the floor space under the desk was occupied, so he contented himself with chaffing his colleagues on their timidity.

"The next night there were no bombs, but somebody tapped the constable on the shoulder, and he beat all records for the dive under the desk, where he found himself alone."

Ambassador Averill Harriman arranged an appointment for me to see the Archbishop of Canterbury, Dr. Geoffrey Fisher.

The previous time I was at Lambeth Palace I was ushered into the great parlor, a palatial room, where the tables had to be large enough for the great silver tea service: the tea pot alone was twelve inches in diameter, with the cream pitcher and sugar bowl of like dimensions. There were very handsome Oriental carpets on the floor. Large windows overlooked the garden and the Thames with its heavy dark barges and smaller craft. When I had tea with Lord Lang, the former Archbishop of Canterbury, he gave me tea in a small library with a coal fire burning cheerfully in the grate. A pretty maid in white cap and apron passed the thin bread and butter, the scones, the plum jam and fruit cake. But this time as I came through the big iron gates leading into the courtyard with the bright green English grass very wet under foot, I had to knock several times on the huge door of the palace before it opened and there was the Archbishop himself! War and bombing had impoverished Great Britain as it may impoverish us, but as I write she is once more on her feet. The Archbishop greeted me and took my umbrella, then showed me into a medium sized room which then seemed to me to be rather bare but this was not 1955.

"You may not know that the palace has been bombed and that now I receive here and I sleep down stairs near the kitchens."

His Grace, the Archbishop is of average height with a dome-like head, keen blue eyes and a jutting nose.

I came to the point at once as men in high places have an immense amount of business to attend to.

He asked me how I expected co-operation from Hindus when they did not believe in God and had hundreds of sects.

"But they do believe in God, your Grace."

"Not in a personal God."

"But I a Christian, do not believe in a personal God. I should not dare so to circumscribe that Being we call God."

"Our Lord has described God to us," said he.

"I cannot remember any particular description," but thought to myself I must read the New testament over again, and continued

"To me a flower expresses God."

"Would you think you knew a person if you saw only his nose?"

But right here I decided the Archbishop could floor me with logic; that I had better retire from the field so I showed him some of the letters given me by other religious dignitaries and said I was going to see the Pope.

"I will be very frank with you. These men promise nothing; they are merely being polite to you."

"I like honesty and frankness, your Grace."

"The Pope, naturally will also consult with the Curiae. Even if the leaders could agree on such a day of fasting and prayer, it would take at least five years to organize it so that the masses could take an understanding part in it. In fifty years there might be a possibility of such co-operation. Dr. Temple worked very hard on merely Christian co-operation, but little was accomplished. If you will excuse me now, I have many letters to write."

I got up and asked for my umbrella. The Archbishop could not find it but at last it was found in a corner of the room. As I went to the door with him, I said, "May I quote you as saying that we might succeed in fifty years?"

He agreed that I might.

I went away wondering what had been accomplished, and why I had come all the way to the palace in this drizzling rain, only to be told that my mission could not be accomplished for fifty years. How little I knew of the slow processes of trying to get cooperation.

Two days later I wrote Archbishop Fisher that I had been grateful for the time he had given me since I knew what heavy responsibilities he bore, but I hoped he would at least wish me well in my difficult endeavor. This is his answer, and a very kind one.

LAMBETH PALACE, S.E.
4th June, 1946

My dear Countess,

Thank you for your letter, which I found awaiting me when I got back from Canterbury this week. I am sorry that our conversation had to be hurried. You have lived with this idea and given yourself to it for a long time and I am afraid you may have thought my comments somewhat abrupt. I have, as you know, serious doubts as to the practicability and even as to the desirability of the particular proposal which you have in mind. My own view is that to such problems a much longer and slower approach is necessary, and I told you something of the movements now in progress which are perhaps the first sure steps of the journey. At the same time, please be assured that I deeply appreciate your own great concern for a spiritual advance of an inclusive kind. That you should be pressing this upon religious leaders in various parts of the world is altogether good.

Yours sincerely,
Geoffrey Cantuar

Three and a half years later I had this further note from Archbishop Fisher:

LAMBETH PALACE
London, S.E.1
4th January, 1950

Dear Comtesse,

I well remember the time when you came to Lambeth and we had a talk together, and of course I remember the general subject of our talk though I cannot remember at all what I said. I do not suppose that I said anything that ought not to be published, and if you can trust your memory I am quite willing that you should make use of our conversation.

I see Myron Taylor from time to time and discuss the same kind of propositions with him as I discussed with you. There can be no spectacular steps towards co-operation between religious leaders, but sympathy and co-operation both grow.

Yours sincerely,
Geoffrey Cantuar

CHAPTER 4

TO PARIS

I took the train to Dover. The crossing was not rough, but what a sight was Calais! Ruins; here and there a building, but almost none undamaged. I saw nothing like it in England. Some temporary low tin shacks received our luggage and ourselves as we went through the customs. The porters were old or very young. The 400,000 prisoners of war were coming back, but in such poor physical condition that they could not do heavy work. I had got some francs in England for tips, so I was soon in a first-class carriage, with an English woman opposite. She looked at the ruins and said,

"We have not been told how dreadfully France has been bombed."

"No, we in America have not been told, either. It has always been the destruction in England that our press has written about. I wonder why?"

She did not know. Perhaps our Government thought Great Britain a more powerful ally than France, so encouraged the press to keep Great Britain before our people as needing the most help.

It was early spring. My heart took this country into its embrace. Beloved in childhood, beloved through my dear French husband, beloved now in the autumn of my life. I could almost have kissed the gray stone Norman farm houses, the blossoming fruit trees, the earth itself. Tears came to my eyes and blurred the countryside as though with rain.

At the gare St. Lazare a porter took my valises and heavier bags slung together on a leather strap on his shoulders. The French porters all wear a wide canvas belt as a protection against hernia. I was taken to the customs, and as there were only two women officers for all of us from the boat train, it was a very slow process. Finally I joined my cries for service with those of a Frenchman who kept repeating,

"J'ai un taxi qui m'attend!"

Later I learned why he had kept a taxi waiting—a peroxide blonde at the train. At last my luggage was marked, and the porter started with me to find a taxi.

"We must hurry, Madame, if you wish to get a taxi."

So we hurried; but when we got out of the station we saw just one taxi, with people getting into it. The porter hurried across from the station and asked the people to let me have a seat in their taxi; but "Non," and they drove off. We began looking up and down the street, but not even a horse and carriage was to be seen.

"Get busy, porter!"

"But, Madame, there are none."

That porter was not making himself useful, and I told him so.

"I can't get a taxi if there aren't any."

Just then a young fellow of sixteen or seventeen came up and asked me if I wanted him to take my valises in the Metro to my hotel. I saw nothing else to do, so I said yes. He buckled a long strap around the two valises, and swinging them over one shoulder, one in front and the other behind, he took a box in one hand and I took the two handbags and the umbrella. We got down into the Metro, tramping through two long corridors, and were about to board the train, when an agent-de-ville came up to my porter and asked him roughly by what right he was carrying my valises.

"You have no porters' badge."

"I don't care whether he has or not," said I. "He is getting me to my hotel."

"Show me your identity card," said the policeman, paying no attention to me. The boy took it out, and the policeman said roughly,

"Follow me!"

"But," I said, "what am I to do with my luggage?"

"That's not my affair." And off he went. By this time I was very tired and rather upset, wondering what on earth I could do. I appealed to a strong-looking young man waiting for his train, and asked if he wouldn't help me with the valises, as I couldn't possibly carry them all. He smiled sweetly, and said it would make him late for dinner. There were people moving all about me, but not one showed the slightest concern. I asked a strange little man with veiled eyes if he would help me.

"I am late now, Madame, but I will go upstairs again and get you a porter."

I saw three policemen talking near me, and went up to them. I can speak French fluently and gesticulate as do the French.

"Have you no hearts?"

"But how now, Madame?" said one.

"But look now, my two large valises, the box and these two handbags! How am I to get them to my hotel tonight when you take away the young man who was carrying them for me?"

"Ah! But it was not a regular porter. But Madame, you don't know how these boys behave. They push you into the Metro, shut the door, and go off with your valises. An old woman has just lost her bag here in this manner. They are *voyous*, these young men!"

"The one I had looked honest."

"Oh, ho! Looked honest! Do I not look honest?"

"Yes; are you not honest?"

"Not always," and he winked at me, while the others laughed.

Just then my little man—a real friend—came down into the Metro with a tall, hollow-cheeked man.

"Here is a man, Madame, who will carry your luggage."

"How good of you; thank you. May I pay you?"

"No, no, certainly not." And he got on to the Metro.

"But you have no porter's badge," said one of the three police.

"Now, really you're not going to take this man away, too? If you do, you'll have to carry the luggage yourselves." They laughed.

The man said, "But Messieurs, you *know* me."

"But that does not give you the right to be a porter."

"For the love of God!" I said.

"But you *know* me," repeated the man.

"Well, yes, it's true, we know you; eh bien, zut! Take Madame's valises." And so we were allowed to get into the Metro.

We got out at Concorde, and I tried to get a taxi, as the valises were heavy; but there were none. There were very few taxis since the drivers were allowed only fifteen gallons of gasoline a day, which many of them sell on the black market because that way they make more money. So the thin man carried the two large valises and the box of food for friends, and I carried the two handbags. We trudged along the Rue de Rivoli, turned down the Rue Cambon, and then to the right on the Rue St. Honore. We found the Hotel de France et Choiseul, and dropped all the luggage at the feet of the concierge. The thin man asked if I had any chocolate for his three children. (His breath smelled of liquor.) I knew that chocolate could be sold at a good profit. I had to take everything out of my handbag to find the chocolate for "the three children," and by that time I was so tired that I wanted to cry. But all things have an end,

57

and I was welcomed by the proprietor, who had known me for many years. He showed me a suite, bedroom, bath, and parlor for five dollars a day. There were few people in that hotel in 1946 except American Army men. Somehow I got to bed.

Marcelle, who is a fine novelist and brilliant lecturer, and my dear friend, came to me the next morning. She threw her arms around me and kissed me on both cheeks.

"At last! How long it has been with this frightful war!"

I had brought her a blue raincoat, which she at once tried on; she looked at herself in the mirror, then hugged me again, and danced around the table.

"I look younger already; I shall wear it all the time."

She then told me of the inroads the Communists had made in France. They have all the money they can spend. They promise the people everything. They send them wheat, which has to be paid for. They control the radio and the press.

"Why don't the Americans publish what *they* are doing for France? The people are told only what the U.S.S.R. does for France. You can see the great placards and signs everywhere. We are not strong enough now to stand alone. It is a choice between Russia and the United States. Why does not America tell our people what she is doing for them?"

Later I spoke to Ambassador Caffery. He answered:

"It is because the Communists control the radio and much of the press, and the French people are afraid to stand out against the Russians. They fear reprisals if the U.S.S.R. should take over France. The industrialists are for us, but are taking no chances in case the U.S.S.R. and not the United States should win. We need money for propaganda. We should have to pay to get notices in the papers. Congress does not give us the money for publicity. Our Secretary of State, Dean Acheson, has asked Congress for funds to spend on this very thing. He wants the facts known of what

America is doing in different parts of the world, but so far Congress has refused the funds." (When I got back to America, I saw several Senators and explained this need.)

"The strongest bulwark against Communists in France is the Catholic Church. She works unremittingly. We are fortunate in having the Catholic Church on our side," explained Ambassador Cafferey.

"I imagine that is why the Communists hate the Catholic Church," I said.

It was difficult not to eat off the black market. There was a small one-room restaurant near my hotel, with no more than seven tables fairly close together. I used to go there before the war, because the food was good but not expensive, with a simple bill of fare, on the order of a *plat du jour*, with little choice. I tried the door, wondering if the restaurant was still running—and sure enough, Mme. Bernard was behind the counter to take in the money, just as in 1938, dressed in black, of course, and a good deal stouter. Her husband, a gentle-faced man, did the cooking upstairs.

I was welcomed with enthusiasm.

"It is so good to see old customers come back after this dreadful war. I had an officer quartered on me all during the occupation. He did no harm, but he used to bore me with praises of Hitler. I used to tell him he could not expect me to love Hitler—that I despised him. 'Madame, be careful what you say. I might have to report you to the police.' 'Then don't talk to me of your Fuhrer, and I shan't be tempted to speak ill of him.'

"In 1942 this officer asked me if I thought the Americans would come into the war. 'But they are in now. They are sending the Allies armaments, oh, the best, and in such enormous quantities.' He turned white with fear. 'You do not think they will fight, do you, Madame?' 'I hope so; they did before.' He looked quite sick, and did not speak to me of Hitler any more. I was content, as I have a quick tongue and might have gone too far."

"What about the black market, Madame?"

"We all use it. How could we live otherwise? I know it should not be, but one cannot see one's children suffering for lack of food—now, can one?"

"But what about the people who are too poor to buy in the black market?"

She shrugged. "Oh, well, it is difficult for them."

It did not seem to occur to her that those who used the black market were vampires, sucking the blood of the very poor as though they were literally at their throats, sucking out their life. When shall we feel for others as we do for ourselves? When shall we observe the second great commandment, "Love thy neighbor as thyself?"

It was cold that afternoon, but there was a patch of sun just inside the gates of the Tuilleries opposite the Rue de Castiglione. I sat myself down on a metal chair, and my mind went back to Paris when I was a child of four. We had a negro nurse, Caroline, who had been my sister Delia's wet nurse in Georgia. We were two rather lonely little strangers, who were led up and down the Tuilleries Gardens along a walk just off the Rue de Rivoli. I remember how sad I used to feel for no reason. I must have sensed the horrors of the Revolution and the guillotine, that still vibrate in the old palace, and even in the iron railings round the gardens.

Sometimes these two little girls with flaxen hair used to whip tops down the Champs Elysees, or roll their hoops, or watch the guignol or puppet show. We had only ourselves to play with.

One afternoon we were crossing the Rue de Rivoli from the Tuileries at the Rue de Castigilone. Caroline was holding us by the hand, and had got us to the second safety zone.

The traffic was heavy with horses and carriages. I decided that if I ran to the sidewalk as fast as I could, I'd beat the traffic. I snatched my hand from Caroline's, who was not expecting such a sudden move, and without looking, darted across the street. Just at the corner a carriage struck me, knocked me down, and a wheel ran over my right leg. I still can see the crowd around me, as I held on to my leg, while my little sister Delia wept loudly. I did not cry—I seldom cried as a child. So my sister was supposed to be the injured child, and a sergeant-de-ville carried her to the American apothecary's across the Rue de Castiglione, and Caroline helped me. The apothecary gave Delia gum drops to stop her crying. We had an apartment across the street, so when we got back there I was put in my crib. How I wished my mother would come home! And why did I not get any gum drops?

I took a day to go to Poictiers, where Dr. Pierre Perier was coming from his home in Bordeaux to spend a few hours with me. We had both worked in the same hospital in Dinard in 1914, and we were good friends. In 1927 I had seen him for a few hours when my two eldest daughters and I had hired a car and driven along the Riviera. I knew he had heart trouble brought on from being gassed at the front in 1915. He had been decorated for courage under fire in the front lines.

It was spring, and I watched the fields stretching to the horizon. What colors! Carpets of blood-red poppies, yellow mustard, blue cornflowers, patches of grayish-green grass and jade green, the red earth not yet planted. Now I saw more masses of blue and purple flowers, and always the red poppies, like those I'd seen and written about in 1915, a week after my husband's death.

FRENCH POPPIES

To Alain

Red poppies bloom
In May and June,
Dear Heart,
Red poppies!
Flowers of Lethe,
Flowers of sleep.

Who put that wreath
Of poppies red
About thy head?
Was it God's hand?
To close thine eyes
From all surprise,
To give thee sleep?

They lie blood red
About thy head,
Dear Heart;
I may not move them
From their place,
To bring the light
To that dear face
That lies in sleep,
Deep sleep

Red poppies bloom
In May and June
In one long life;
And there men sleep,
And women weep, and weep.

Where were the farmers? I could see only one peasant
mowing. Farther on a man was plowing with two horses.

There were few horses; the Germans took all the best ones. My friend Marguerite told me how difficult it was for the women left alone on the farms with the children to keep the farms going at all, and yet they had to live. Some of the men, when they came back from German prisons, complained because the farms had run down. They could not seem to realize that with only old horses—and even these were hard to find—and most of the cattle taken, one woman with young children had neither the strength nor the means to farm as in peacetime, when their men were at home.

Gradually the landscape changed to green wheat fields, with grapes planted between.

I noticed the man opposite me had an empty sleeve. His face was sensitive; his hair graying; he was thin. In another corner sat a fat, well-dressed man, probably a product of the black market; never a prisoner of war; doubtless pulled wires to keep out of the army. The time may come when it will be unsafe to be fat, when others are lean.

Poictiers! More than half destroyed!—but there was Pierre waiting for me. I recognized his Basque bêret, and his smile.

He took me to a cafe, where we had lunch, and then we talked first of our families; then of France.

"This is what is happening in our part of France. I have a farm which we let to a farmer and his family, he to get half the produce of the farm, and I the other half as rental. For years we have been on the best of terms, and I have helped this family at different times. Then a good-looking young man comes to our district—no one knows from where. He marries the farmer's daughter, and soon the old friendly feeling toward me changes. I am treated like an outsider. Then I am told they want to buy my farm. I refuse, as we are fond of it—we have had it many years. The farmer tells me he will no longer pay rent in produce, that he wants to buy. I tell him I won't sell, and that he had better leave, and I shall find someone else to whom to rent the farm. He tells me he will shoot me if I come near the farm to dispossess him. I don't dare go near the farm, my own property, as I have a quick temper and blood might be shed. They will probably get my farm in the end for a sou, as they will ask the Mayor to put it up for auction, and he won't dare refuse; no one will bid but my farmer, and he will get it. This is not one case, but one of many. The Communists want a revolution of our peasant farmers—and we shall have one, I feel sure."

After lunch we sat near the station together, and he held my hand. We both knew we should not meet again in this life. He died the next year of heart failure.

His Excellency Archbishop Richard Cushing had given me a letter to His Eminence, Cardinal Suhard, Archbishop of Paris. Monsignor John J. Wright, now Bishop Wright, had told me of the many illegitimate babies in the aftermath of war in France, so I had a valise full of baby clothes for the Cardinal's poor. This I took with me in a taxi to His Eminence on the Rue Barbet de Jouy, where I had formerly been received by Cardinal Verdier, a wise and holy man. The street is a quiet one on the Rive Gauche, not far from the Invalides.

The valise was taken by the concierge across the paved court enclosed by high walls, like so many of the homes of an earlier royal France. Up one flight of red-carpeted stairs to an anteroom, where I waited with the valise. I did not wait long. His Eminence soon came, a benign old man, with the kindest, sparkling eyes. I kissed his ring—was it a ruby or an amethyst?—an archbishop wears an amethyst, but this dear old man was also a cardinal. He led the way to the sitting room, upholstered in gray and red; and I told him in French why I had come. I told him that the Archbishop of Canterbury thought it would take fifty years for the leaders of the great faiths to agree on the same day of fasting and prayer to the One Father of us all—in these days of wars, rumors of wars, famine, and earthquakes.

"Do you not think, Your Eminence, that with the help of God it might be done in less time?"

"I do not think it would take fifty years, my child. Go on working, as hard as you can, and God will finish the work."

"Your Eminence, this is not just for Christians, but for all those who believe in God. After all, we are His children; He made us all, even if some pray to Him differently."

"Yes, my child, we are all His children. And you—do you believe in God?"

"Surely, Your Eminence."

"Do you believe in our Lord, Jesus Christ?"

"But certainly I do."

"Then all is well with you."

Then I told him what I tell to few, my visions of the Christ.

"Do you think the Holy Father will see me when I get to Rome?"

"Yes, I think he will."

"Will you give me your benediction, Your Eminence? I need help in this task."

"Yes, my child."

I knelt, with my hat off, while he blest me,—and from those hands I knew that I was indeed blest.

I arose to go, and His Eminence said,

"My door is always open to you. Come and see me when you come back to Paris."

And so I left him, with renewed hope of a conciliation between those different leaders who, each in his way, tried to guide his flock to the Father, but I shall not see His Eminence again in this life as he died the next year.

CHAPTER 5

TO ROME

Have you flown in an ATC army plane? From Paris to Rome, I sat on a tin bench running along two-thirds of each side of the plane. Forward there are no seats, but the parachutes are piled upon the floor. If you try to lean back in your metal seat you encounter a sharp edge, so you lean forward. I asked for a parachute bundle to lean against, as we were taking off, especially as I had been given instruction before getting into the plane on how to put one on, how to jump, how to count ten before pulling the metal handle of the cord. I could not have my parachute, though I said it would be far handier to have it near me if I had to jump than to have it in the front end of the plane. But once we got well up in the air one of the three women in the plane moved to the front where it was warmer and curled up on one of the parachute bundles. She evidently knew her way around. The rest of the passengers were army officers, except for two priests from Australia, two Russians, and a young man whom the woman on the bundles had called Jeffrey. He was reading a book of French poetry. Gradually all the men stretched out on the benches, lay on the floor at our feet, or curled upon the parachutes. These they moved if it pleased them; so evidently one waits to take off before making practical use of the parachutes. Every commercial plane should of course have parachutes, just as a ship has life preservers, and drills on how to put on the life preserver and how to find one's lifeboat. It is absurd of the airplane companies not to have them for fear people will be nervous and won't fly. On the contrary, they will feel the companies are providing for their safety, in case of accident; and we are having more accidents rather than fewer. The public should insist on safety, as they did after the great loss of life at sea on the *Titanic*.

The American Express Company in Paris had telegraphed the American Express in Rome to meet me at the Ciampino Airport some miles outside of Rome to take me to the hotel they had chosen for me, but no American Express agent could be found; just as there had been none to meet the 10:30 P.M. boat-train when I arrived in London from Southampton, though Thomas Cook & Sons' agent was on hand to help *their* passengers. My Italian consisted of only a few words, and I could not hear myself telephoning in Italian; but Captain Hanson, who had spoken to me on the plane, saw me wandering about alone, after I had missed the bus to Rome while I looked for the American Express agent, and he asked me if he could be of any use.

"Could you be of use? Heaven sent you to me. What shall I do? There is no American Express agent to tell me what hotel I'm to go to, and now I've missed the bus. What shall I do?"

"Why don't you telephone to our Embassy and ask them to send an Embassy car to get you?"

"What a marvelous idea! Will you get them on the 'phone for me?"

Captain Hanson got Ambassador Kirk's secretary very quickly, and I told her my predicament.

"I was just going to my hotel, but I'll send the Embassy car and arrange for you to stay at the Excelsior Hotel for two nights until you are straightened out."

"How good of you! I thought I should have to sleep on a bench at the airport."

Captain Hanson and I talked until the Embassy car came. I learned that he was from Minneapolis. He was captain of a crew servicing army planes. He'd enjoyed Paris—who doesn't? But he wanted more responsibility and had been sent to Rome; he did not know for how long. I told him a little of my reason for being in Rome; and then I thought, what shall I do for this polite young man?

"Do you know many people in Rome?" I asked him.

"No one yet."

"Would you care to dine with me when I find out which is my hotel?"

"I'd like that very much."

He gave me his name and address at the airport where he was to work, and when the Embassy car arrived he put me into it and off I went.

The Excelsior Hotel, once a palace, is situated on one of the hills of Rome near one of the parks. The entrance hall is enormous, with a tiled floor and very high ceilings. I was shown a lovely, palatial double bedroom with bath, cool tiled floors, at very low rates. After resting before dinner, I went down to the very large dining room, which was full of army men and their wives. We had American food, which is not exciting. I don't like our American bakers' white bread, chemically whitened and softened and tasteless, without the germ which is the life of the wheat. At breakfast I was given Post Toasties. In England, oatmeal, or "porridge," as the British call it, is always served; untreated oatmeal with skimmed milk will support life, as the Scotch know, with no other food. But try living on Post Toasties!

After breakfast I went to the American Express Company to find out why I had not been met, and at what hotel a room had been reserved for me. As is customary, the Company hires Italians in Italy, French people in France, Indians in India, etc. to run their offices, which is no doubt the

68

reason we do not get American efficiency except at home.

I asked the good-looking Italian in charge why I had not been met at the airport.

"But your plane arrived after office hours, Countess."

"That is no excuse. You should have sent a man out on the bus no matter what the hour. If it had not been for my Embassy sending a car for me when in despair I telephoned, I should have had to sit up all night at the airport. I think very little of the way you run this office."

"Excuse, Countess, I regret exceedingly. We have a room for you at the Hotel Regina, where you will be very comfortable."

I moved there the next day, and found it a quiet, rather small hotel, with very good food. In 1946 there were no tourists, only our Army, Navy, and Air Force men, newsmen, and an occasional person like myself bent on special work, so the hotels were thinly populated.

I had a letter from Archbishop Richard J. Cushing of Boston to Monsignor Thomas F. Markham, and he arranged for me to see one of the papal secretaries of state, Monsignor Carroll, who was to help me see the Pope.

From the hotel I took a victoria to the Vatican. The old driver kept up a continual cooing of "ahs" to his steed, I suppose to encourage it to trot now and then. The creature looked well fed and well cared for, but fell into a walk on the slightest rise of the road. Since I had engaged the chariot by the hour it occurred to me that the driver was not discouraging this deliberateness; but one does not hurry in Rome.

We drove through avenues of magnolias and oleanders. A strong and intoxicating perfume came from the magnolias, but there are other smells in Rome.

I had forgotten the beauty of the stately houses in Rome—burnt umber and old gold. I had forgotten the procession of trees on the avenues, with their color and life and beauty;

and the pines, that rise tall and slender umbrella-like with branches only at the top. I had forgotten the immense semi-circle of pillars as you go into the first huge enclosure of the Vatican. Those old architects gave their kings and popes space in which to move. Inside I certainly did a lot of moving from one great hall to another; and up wide staircases not built for me, but for the stride of tall men. Of course I was stopped at the first entrance, my passport taken from me, and my life history inscribed on a printed form, as though I were coming into a strange country—and so I was, the earthly domain of the Holy Father, the Papal State.

How was I to find Monsignor Carroll in this huge palace? I, who could say little more than "non parlare Italiano." I was waved in this direction and that; and might still be wandering like a lost soul up and down great stairways if a young man had not taken pity on me and shown me an elevator.

On an upper floor I showed the letter to Monsignor Carroll to a concierge. He telephoned and then waved me to wait in a further room. After half an hour I went back to the concierge, where I found two other Americans also looking for Monsignor Carroll. Had they bribed the concierge? For them Monsignor Carroll soon appeared. He seemed much annoyed that he had not been notified of my arrival. He led me back to a small reception room. He was a youngish man with a direct, frank look, and genial, friendly manners.

"I was not told you were waiting. I'm so sorry."

I explained why I hoped for a private audience with the Holy Father.

"This is interesting. Why should not the religious leaders co-operate. It certainly would be a strong move, if only they could be induced to. You must see the Holy Father. I feel sure he will see you. I will notify you of the day and hour."

But I decided to get the help of Ambassador Myron C.

Taylor, since I did not want to delay too long my trips to Egypt and India.

At the Embassy near my hotel I found that Ambassador Taylor was away, but his aide, Franklin C. Gowen, had heard from our Under Secretary of State Dean Acheson, and was quite ready to arrange for a private audience with the Pope.

"Will you give me the object of your mission? That is customary when asking for a private audience."

He wrote it down as I gave it.

"I think this can be arranged in two or three days. I will let you know. Where are you staying?"

"At the Hotel Regina."

"Let me give you directions on how to get to the Pope's reception room, since the Vatican is large."

"I've already wandered a mile there in trying to see Monsignor Carroll."

"I will draw a small plan for you."

"This will save me many steps. Thank you so much, Mr. Gowan."

"Come and tell me what results from your audience."

"I will; thank you again. Good-bye."

Three days later the telephone rang, and I was told that the Pope would see me at eleven Tuesday morning.

I am still amazed at the size of the Vatican, though I do not think the architect succeeded in giving the impression of proportions as do the ancient Egyptian temples like Karnac. Nevertheless, the many large rooms are individually more impressive than those at the Louvre. In 1901 I was in the Vatican with my mother and sister to attend an audience of the Holy Father for perhaps three hundred Hungarian peasants. We had bought our way in from one of the men who make money from showing the Vatican to travelers.

We entered the great hall, with its life-size paintings of

71

the Massacre of St. Bartholomew. I was personally interested in the massacred corpse of the Great Admiral de Coligny being carried on a stretcher through the streets of Paris to incite the populace to more murders of the Huguenots; the man I loved, to whom I was then engaged, was a direct descendant of the Admiral through his grandmother. His family was now Catholic, since even Henry IV had become Catholic to save his life and to become king. *Une couronne vaut bien une messe.*

The ceilings of this great palace were decorated with historical life-size portraits of the famous prelates of the Catholic Church—Catholic kings, who had increased the temporal power of the Church; which is human, for all temples made with hands naturally give their builders a feeling of importance. Yet how childish we are to think *our* temples will last; when every land has crumbled ruins of earlier palaces and temples.

Great rooms had walls lined with crimson brocade, picturing Peter's crossed keys—for here, it is said, lived Peter's successors. Perhaps the simple fisherman would wonder at this mansion made with hands; even as other wise men of other religions wonder at the excrescences small men have overlaid on their wise teachings, until at last the truth is suffocated and humanity is a flock of sheep without a shepherd. Then crimes grow and love dies, until we are faced—as now—with viciousness, torture, wholesale murder, despair.

But of course we must remember, as Father LaFarge pointed out to me, that the luxurious living of some of the Popes is not true today, in spite of the Vatican itself. Frugality is both urged and practiced.

Any great, world-wide organization, like the Politburo and the Roman Church, can be no stronger than its weakest link. How to have no weak links? There is no way, as long as human beings are imperfect. Both the Communists and the Roman Church aim to control all human beings; the first because the fourteen men in the Kremlin have the power complex and their egos demand it, the other because the Roman Church believes its way to heaven is the only way. Therefore these two powerful organizations hate each other, and are at war to the death. Even so, this struggle must not lead to murderous wars.

Thoughts like these had come to me more than once in the thirty years I had been working for peace among men. Now, as I made my way through the palace of the popes to beg Pope Pius XII to call the religious leaders of the world together in a conclave for unity of spiritual purpose to stem the power of the unspiritual, retrograde forces led by the Politburo, as they had been formerly led by Hitler, I wondered if the Archbishop of Canterbury was right, and the decision must be made not by the Pope, but by the Curiae. Anyway, the attempt had to be made.

In the immense hall, its ceilings covered with paintings, I asked one of the Swiss Guards how to reach the Pope's reception room. (These men were dressed as they were three hundred years ago—in bright blue and yellow, the doublet slashed to show scarlet, as were the knee breeches, leather boots to the knee, the whole uniform a riot of color.) The tall Swiss Guard showed me to the anteroom where I was to wait. I asked him quizzically in French if he were really Swiss.

"But naturally, Madame."

"I did not think the Swiss were still hired by the Vatican."

"And why not, Madame?"

"Why, it's been three hundred years!"

"Yes, and more."

"I can't imagine a custom like this going on and on in America."

"But this is not America, Madame. It is the Catholic Church."

73

"C'est épatant!" I smiled and went on. In another large room I awaited my time.

At last a man, dressed in crimson satin knee breeches and a crimson ecclesiastical gown, led me through two more large empty rooms, into a small one with a desk, behind which sat His Holiness. He motioned me to a chair at his left hand; but I first knelt and kissed his sapphire ring.

His Holiness, in a white robe with a round white skull cap on his head, looked as white as his gown, and very frail. He had been ill, and I thought of the war, and the difficulties of keeping his flock together in Nazi and Fascist countries. He asked me where I came from, and when I said "America," he smiled, almost the only smile during the twenty minutes we talked. I knew he spoke French and English, but I thought French seemed a little easier for him; so we spoke in French. I told him that I hoped he could lead the world to a spirit of unity but with each religion holding to its own dogma. In his encyclicals he had several times spoken of the need for the unity of mankind.

"The times are too chaotic, too difficult for any such move. We must wait till many questions have been straightened out."

"But, Holy Father, if the children of God could become conscious of their fundamental unity, would not these difficult questions resolve themselves more easily and quickly?"

"It is too difficult to get the leaders of religions to agree; what we must do is to pray much and often."

"Yes, Holy Father, that must be done always, as our Lord told us, but God helps those who help themselves. His Eminence Cardinal Suhard told me in Paris that we must work as hard as we could, then God would finish the work."

"The times are too difficult. We must solve first some of the questions of today."

"But Holy Father, we need a drastic change to help men

74

of good will to unite against the evil and atheism which work so constantly against us."

"We must say many prayers; that will help."

"Yes, but if we could once pray together all over the world, would not God be glad to see His children pray to Him together?"

"In time this will happen, since our Lord told us there would one day be but one religion. We must pray unceasingly."

I looked into those inscrutable black eyes, feeling that we might go on getting nowhere for another twenty minutes. I got up, and he gave me a white box in which was a mother-of-pearl rosary strung on a gilt chain. I thanked him for this and for seeing me, knelt and kissed his ring, and backed out of the small room. The Pope had said all he could at that time, but it was he who made the first move in 1952 toward Islam. He has proved a great and good man under exhausting pressures in our world's most critical years. He is a bulwark against materialistic Communism and I pray earnestly that he keeps his health and strength.

The chamberlin showed me out. I told him how handsome he looked in his beautiful crimson suit. He was pleased and showed it.

"It is handsome, is it not?" he said.

I made this gesture because I was discouraged by my audience, and to give some one else pleasure was an antidote.

The next day I went to see Franklin Gowen to report on the audience.

"I feel as if I had failed, Mr. Gowen; yet the idea will spread. The *Boston Globe* will help as a report of this audience will be published and Boston at least will know something of it. The Archbishop of Canterbury told me the Curiae would be consulted and I have at least one cardinal who is in favor, Cardinal Suhard, Archbishop of Paris. I feel this job has to be done. I am only one instrument and not a very good one."

"It takes time for anything so difficult to get even a start. Where do you go next?"

"To Cairo, to see the president of Al Azhar University. The Egyptian Ambassador told me he was the spiritual leader of Islam. I want to thank you for your help."

I had seen His Holiness surrounded by all the grandeur and beauty that the imagination of man has devised. As I again pass through the palatial rooms in memory, with their great paintings, the crimson brocade-covered walls, the Swiss Guards, I see also a child in a cave in Bethlehem with His mother and father and the gentle domestic animals. The child needed no palace to enhance the beauty of its spirit; that Spirit chose to appear first in the humblest of dwellings, and His disciples were humble men. He taught humility, and lived His teachings—even washing the feet of His disciples. Why do we, who profess to follow Him, build great cathedrals in His honor, instead of breathing on the flame of His Spirit in our hearts that we might love one another as He loves us, that the flame might burn clear and strong and bright, not a weak and flickering light that often goes out altogether in the dense murk of our time?

"In Him was light; and the light was the life of men."

Have not material possessions weakened all the Christian Churches, Protestant and Greek Orthodox, as well as the Roman, and the Buddhist, Mohammedan—all temples, all religions? Everywhere man finds it easier to spend his strength and his riches on temples made with hands, than in the more arduous, self-sacrificing work of building up the temple of his own body and soul for the Divine Spirit to dwell in.

In 1948 I read again *The Treasure House of the Living Religions* by Robert Ernest Hume, M.A., Ph.D., Yale

University; Docteur de l'Université de Strasbourg. Translated into Spanish, 1933. Then my eyes were opened and I remembered the Holy Father's reminding me that our Lord said that one day we should have but one religion. It was then I went to the Voice of America with a leaflet of the two great commandments as given in all the great religions and asked that our fundamental unity should be broadcast to the world. But I was told the Voice never broadcast anything that had not appeared in a newspaper or that some prominent person, like Mrs. Franklin D. Roosevelt, had not mentioned in her daily letter. One should not argue with the laws of the Medes and the Persians, so I wrote to Mrs. Roosevelt, sending her the two great commandments and asked her if she would not mention them so the Voice could broadcast them? But she refused. I then went back to the Voice of America and asked if the broadcast could be made if the U.N. would first broadcast the two great commandments. "Oh yes!" that would be O.K.

Now I had no idea how I was to get the U.N. to do this, but the order had been flashed to me, I see now, and anyhow I went to work.

It took me ten months to convince the U.N. that these commandments were not controversial and I got the help of Dr. Harold C. Urey and Dr. Henry Smith Leiper, then the Executive Secretary of the National Council of the Churches of Christ in America, who wrote letters to the U.N. hoping "It" would broadcast the two great commandments.

They were broadcast and then of course the Voice of America could safely follow suit.

Dr. Hume is dead but I am sure he is well pleased that his most important work should have gone to the world over the air, to the ends of the earth—to the glory of God. And that His children should realize that they could worship Him as they pleased, but that they were one in love for Him and for each other.

77

My time in Rome was not entirely given over to the audience with Pope Pius. In the State Department I had been advised to give business as my reason for wishing to travel; so I went to the Government agency for ball bearings, as I had in Paris; since with dollars scarce, the Italian Government had to decide who was to have ball bearings and how many.

One afternoon, while I was waiting to be notified when my audience was to be, Captain Hanson came to ask me to go to the opera with him. I hesitated. I did not like opera. People don't really sing when they're dying, or when their hearts are burdened; the singers are fat, and few can act; and I had been obliged to keep an opera box filled for a rich old lady friend for two winters, when opera was given for two weeks in Boston. The old lady always had a box but never asked me to invite guests to fill it till two or three days before the performance; therefore they thought I was asking them to fill in at the last moment. I got very tired of sitting at the telephone for hours trying to fill the old lady's box.

But Captain Hanson looked so disappointed that I thought, "How mean of me; he's trying to be kind; he knows no one else yet to ask; I can bear it." So I accepted.

"I'll call for you at seven and take you to dine at our hotel, which is requisitioned for the Air Force on duty here. The food is American, and good."

I put on a lace dress and tried to look well; I remembered that men want women they take out to "do them proud." He looked pleased when he came for me; and after dinner we drove to the Baths of Caracalla. Who can imagine the beauty that once was there? But we saw beauty there this night, in Verdi's "The Power of Destiny."

The great amphitheatre was filled. At the back is a very great and high wall, built against a hill, and on its top, where runs a road, the poor of the city leaned and listened. Two huge remnants of the broken amphitheatre form the sides of

78

the stage. A new moon and one lone star shone upon us. Strong arc lights drew into relief tall black cypresses and umbrella pines, "The pines of Rome," enhancing the darkness and the gloom.

We sat on raised wooden seats in the warm June night. The music rose and fell; upon the stage, as in the human hearts that saw and listened, the drama of life was played. Near us was a young couple, his arm around her. What did the music and the tragedy of love on the stage do to these two? Music's vibrations swept through the heartstrings of our souls, and we reverberated with our human soul-song.

Captain Hanson told me we must leave before the end in order to be sure of getting a taxi.

"Why not walk, then? It is not far."

"It wouldn't be safe. I could not protect you alone. There are thugs in doorways who jump out on you, knock you down, steal, and, if necessary, knife you. At night two of us always go out together." So we took a taxi.

We had been told over the radio and by CARE that the Italians were starving. I looked carefully as I drove and walked through the streets for signs of starvation, but I did not go into the slums. I watched the poor buying in the open stalls, on an avenue, as they do in Paris, but I saw no wolfish eyes on the food. At the small village of Tivoli, half destroyed by bombs, I saw no thin and haggard people, but neither did I see the fat people I used to see in Italy and France; but among the rich, yes.

What may have been true in wartime is so no longer. Our Government still asks us to help for reasons of state, to keep on friendly terms with our Allies because of Russia and her satellites. I know there are men in government who would have us go on helping for Christian reasons until all our Allies are as well fed as we are; but most of them, I'm afraid, do it for selfish reasons. The Quakers do it for the love of

CHAPTER 6

TO EGYPT

IT WAS in 1943 that I went to see the Minister for Egypt in Washington to try and get a visa, and to find out who was the religious leader of the Mohammedan world.

His Excellency Mahmoud Hassan was courteous, and told me the President of Al Azhar University, Sheik Gazali, was the man for me to see.

"Will you give me a letter to him?"

"There is no need. Our holy men are always willing to discuss religion."

"Will you give me a visa for Egypt?"

"I cannot give you a visa in war time."

"Tell me, Your Excellency, is it because the British will not allow it?"

This was not tactful, and the Minister was not pleased.

"Any time that you bring me word from your Department of State, I will give you a visa immediately from this desk."

"Thank you very much; I'll be coming."

But when the Socialist government was voted in in Great Britain and I could get a visa to Egypt, His Excellency Mahmoud Hassan was no longer Minister to the United States.

Meanwhile I had been to San Francisco in 1945, not to witness the borning of the United Nations, but to get in touch with representatives from the Middle East, for it was the Middle East that would be the scene of the great struggle between Russia and the West.

I saw some dozen of these delegates and met some of the women at a luncheon for "Famous Women." Why I was asked I am not sure, as I am not famous, but it might have been due to Mary Kenney Applegate, who was a secretary at the United Nations Association. I believe she told someone on the committee that I should be asked.

It was the Ambassador to London from Saudi Arabia, His Excellency Sheik Hafiz Wahba, who best understood my effort to get the religious leaders to co-operate. A handsome Arab, not as tall as some, but with an understanding heart. He told me just as Mahmoud Hassan had that I must see the President of Al Azhar University, Sheik Moustafa Abd-el-Razek, as Sheik Gazali was dead; that to him the Mohammedan world turned as leader.

"What you are trying to do is good; the religious leaders should learn to work together so as to bring mankind together in peace."

I saw him again in London in 1946. I noticed the portrait of two lovely girls on the wall. He told me they were his daughters, and love shone in his eyes. It was then that he asked me to go to Palestine to talk to Arab friends of his about the Palestine conflict.

"When you have talked to my friends, go then to the most important Jews. Thus you will get both sides of this question."

This seemed very fair to me, but I asked for a written introduction.

"I never give such things in writing."

"But, Your Excellency, I could not go to these men without a written word from you. They do not know of me." He hesitated, then he said,

"You look honest; I will trust you." And he wrote a few words on his calling card.

I still have it, but I failed to see his friends, as I was taken very ill in Cairo, and after ten days in bed at my friend's home in Alexandria, Justice and Mrs. Jasper Y. Brinton, I decided I'd better fly home. But this was a second instance of an Easterner being more aware of honesty and truth than Westerners. I was buying a Star sapphire in Cairo at Pohoomah Brothers opposite Shephard's Hotel, now destroyed. I had spent two hours looking at Star sapphires for my goddaughter. At last I decided on one, but told the head of the firm that I did not have the money with me, but would bring it the next day.

"Have you not a check, Madame?"

"Yes, but you don't know me."

"We make it our business to read faces. I am sure your check is good."

So I gave him my check for the amount; but in Boston, where I was born, no shop would take my check unless I was an old customer, and even so, I sometimes had to be identified.

In 1946, in early June, I had no trouble getting a visa from the Egyptian Embassy in New York, as I had a letter from His Excellency Mahmoud Hassan; but the Egyptian Consul advised me strongly not to go to Egypt, as conditions were very uncertain and they did not want travelers there at present.

"But I must go."

"Why not go next winter? That is the time to visit Egypt. The climate is then delightful."

"But I must go now, no matter what the climate is. I have a mission to see the Mohammedan religious leader, Sheik Gazali."

"He is now dead, but his successor Sheik Moustafa Abd-el-Razek, President of Al Azhar University, is the man to see."

"This is the man I must see with your help." His whole manner changed.

"This is different; I shall not try to dissuade you. May I ask about your mission?"

"Men are like lost sheep wandering. They need to unite against war. I hope the religious heads will co-operate, and together help their followers to live in peace with each other and the world."

"Madame, this is a noble mission; may you succeed. I will give you your visa now."

At last I had my French and British visas. The Italian visa was simple to get, as some of the Allied troops were still in Italy, and I did not have to pay for it.

From Rome I took a plane at the Ciampino airport to Cairo via Geneva and Athens. Franklin Gowen had arranged this for me. The airport bus at Cairo had gone before I was through the customs, so I had to take a taxi. I was a little nervous, because I spoke no Arabic, it was getting dark, and it was a long time before we even got to Cairo proper; but in spite of my fear of being held for ransom or some other Egyptian (and American) plans for quick money, I did arrive at the Hotel Continental, and told the porter to pay my taxi to avoid discussion. The Continental is a meeting place for East and West, whereas Shephard's Hotel was for Westerners or even more for the British. Shephard's was destroyed during the riots and destruction and deaths in Cairo in 1952, due certainly in most part to Red incitement. The Continental is on a widening of the street and opposite gardens, which made for more coolness. June is hot in Egypt. I was given a large, high-ceilinged room overlooking the street and gardens. The hotel was cool.

I missed the bright-colored gowns and coats of the handsome dragomen who used to stroll the streets of Cairo near the hotels looking for tourists. I remember one in 1934 accosting me. "I hope you remember Ali Mohammed, who was your dragoman last year, my lady?"

I smiled sweetly. "But I wasn't here last year. It was the year before."

He smiled as though he had always known me. "Ah well, my lady, it is never too early to try me," he said quite unabashed, and gave me his card. I was too lazy to send for him, and hired a dragoman from the Continental who was not handsome at all.

Now these men wear full length white gowns which don't always look clean. They wear a broad band of red or green six inches above their waists, and the fez, a high red felt hat without a brim, with a black tassel hanging from the middle of the crown; these are worn indoors and out. The Egyptian women of the lower classes wear black draperies exactly like the blue gown depicted in the pictures of the Mother of Christ. Some of these women wear veils, thick veils that show only the eyes; but this custom is disappearing. A lace veil is worn by the rich cosmopolitan women as a sop to custom, but the face is not hidden. The poor women carry children of two to five years astride on one shoulder, which is much less fatiguing than our way. What patient, melancholy faces these poor Arab women have; there is no light in their eyes or joy, except in those of the young people on the beaches; one does not see the laughing faces we see even in our large cities, and more in our towns and villages.

Cecil B. Lyon, Chargé d'Affaires of our Legation, whose wife was Elsie Grew, Joseph C. Grew's daughter, had a house in Hancock, New Hampshire. Elsie's grandmother and my mother went to school together, and I had played with the three Perry girls in Paris when their mother, Lilla Cabot Perry, and my father William Tudor were studying painting.

Cecil had heard from Acting Secretary of State Dean G. Acheson and was expecting me. I told him I wanted to see the president of Al Azhar University. He said he would arrange it and would let me know the day and hour.

"How is Elsie?" I asked.

"She had to go home, as she was ill with the stomach trouble so many Americans and Europeans get here."

"I'm sorry. How is she now?"

"She got better as soon as she got to Paris, but now she's with her father and mother in Washington. I'm going to ask John Brinton, our cultural attaché, to call for you and take you to see his Excellency the Sheik."

"Brinton? Is he any relation of Justice Jasper Brinton of the Mixed Courts?"

"Yes, his son."

"Do you know the Brintons, Cecil?"

"I see them often at Alexandria, and naturally see John here."

"I'm at the Continental, and shall wait there till I hear from you. Thanks so much for smoothing my way."

"I should like to have you dine with me, even if Elsie is not here to greet you. Could you come tomorrow at nine, if I send my car for you, which can pick up John and a friend of ours?"

"Why, how nice, Cecil! I'd love to come."

"If you could be ready at eight-thirty that will be time enough."

The next morning an Arab in long white robe, broad red belt, and fez brought me my breakfast in my room. I took plenty of time to bathe and dress, and then went to the American Express Company for money. I wandered through the park opposite the Continental and watched the Egyptians, the Arabs, the Negroes, and the Europeans. I could not help noticing how much handsomer these dark-skinned people are than the washed-out white-skinned people. They have a grace of movement and dignity that most of us lack.

I had lunch on the wide, shady veranda in front of the Continental. There were many small tables with polyglot samples of humanity; the fat and rich—for fat is a sign of affluence in lands where the masses struggle not too success-fully to keep from starvation. This was no season for tourists, as it was June and very hot, but there were men in Cairo on business and no doubt for political reasons. I am drawn by beauty in man or woman, and there was a young man not far from me who was not only handsome but beautiful. He must have been from the Middle East, very tall when he got up to leave, with the carriage of a kingly race from the East. His skin was light brown, and his head was as beautiful as a Greek statue's. He stopped and spoke to an older man at another table. His charm was magnetic and he had that rare gift of joy in his smile. I shall never know who he was nor what his fate will be, but I hope he is destined to bring joy and a better life to his people.

I read and rested in my room through the heat of the day and then dressed for dinner. Cecil's car was announced and I went down to it, stopping on the way to pick up John Brinton and pretty Mrs. Bamberger. The night was cool for Egypt, and we were not very long in getting out of the city proper to the road that leads to the pyramids and beyond to Cecil's house. He was at the door to greet us, and with him the British Chargé d'Affaires, James Boker.

We had dinner on the moonlit lawn; the table for five stood on a carpet, and two tall glass shades kept the candles from flickering. Though the pyramids were very near, trees hid them from us.

"I have arranged for you to see Sheik Abd-el-Razek tomorrow, Countess de Pierrefeu, at six o'clock. John will call for you and escort you out to the Sheik's house in Heliopolis."

"How quick you are; and how nice to have you take me, John. Tell me something of the Sheik, Cecil."

"Sheik Moustafa Abd-el-Razek Pacha is the president of the University of Al Azhar of fourteen thousand students, the oldest university of the Middle East and of the Islamic world. Islam looks to him for spiritual leadership."

"I have been told by his Excellency Mahmoud Hassan Pacha in Washington and His Excellency Sheik Hafiz

Wahba, Ambassador from Saudi Arabia to Great Britain, that the president of Al Azhar University was the man for me to see; but I understand that this man has not long been the president."

"No, only two years; but he is said to be more liberal than his predecessor."

"Please tell us what you are doing and why you want to see the Sheik," said Mrs. Bamberger.

I explained the general idea, and was surprised that these four people kept on the subject of religion all through dinner. It was not I who kept it up, it was the others.

"What makes you think you can get the religious leaders to ask their followers to pray together for "Unity in the Spirit?" asked Cecil.

"I am only one of a number of people who are working toward this same end, or much the same. The idea will spread, and you can't kill an idea. But, as I had said to the Pope, it is vitally necessary for all those who believe in God to make a stand together against the Communist atheists. The Communists are undermining the body of humanity like a dreadful disease."

"They are undermining the governments of every country that is not under their dominion; we can see that going on here," said John. "Everywhere in the world—or shall I say in any country that the Politburo feels is of importance to their ultimate domination of the world—this quiet infiltration goes on."

"When it is far enough advanced then the Reds will strike; but it must not be allowed to advance any further," said Cecil.

"The work I am doing is one way to stop this creeping disease. I do not feel it is my work, but the will of God."

"How do you know it is the will of God?" asked John.

"My reason tells me that the Almighty Spirit intends that His creation should be united and 'perfect even as He is perfect'; and yet I can't explain why I do it. I only know it is as though I had been ordered to do it."

"Even I know what she means," said Mrs. Bamberger, "though I'm not doing anything special. There is an inner voice that forces you to; there are spiritual forces that push you."

"You're way over my head," said John.

"Just what does she mean by 'push you'?" said James Boker to me.

"It's on the same principle as a composer's inspiration. My cousin Fred Converse—our American composer, one of the world's giant composers, more appreciated in any part of the world than in his own country—told me that he would hear the music in his head and he had to write it down. It was as if someone outside himself gave him the music; or perhaps it was his superself."

"Yes, that is a possible explanation," commented Boker.

"Cecil, what made you go into the diplomatic service? What makes a Catholic feel sure he has the call to the Church which is a renunciation of the world's pleasure?"

"I really don't know; but in my case I was interested in the possibility of service. The call to the Church must be much the same."

"As a Christian, Madame de Pierrefeu, what is your approach to these leaders of other religions?" asked Mrs. Bamberger.

"Well, I believe in all the great religions. I have done some studying—not much, but enough to convince me that they all teach the fundamental truths of how man should live for his own good and the good of the whole. Every one of the leaders I have talked to has responded to the appeal for spiritual unity—especially as I myself am in sympathy with all the great religions and can speak of them with sympathy. But here we are, under the shadow of the pyramid of Gizeh, which is thought to be the record of history in stone of higher mathematics, of astronomy and the positions of the stars when it was built (which gives us its date), and the evolution of the soul from darkness to light. Cecil, you who live so close to this remarkable monument, do you get any of its vibrations?"

"I had not thought of it in this light, but I shall be more alert to any vibrations it may send me in future. I have heard many theories about it, but not yours on evolution. But do let me show you our house."

We all went in and I was shown the house, which had some fine art objects; but I missed Elsie, whom I had known since she played with my children in Hancock, and I missed a chance to hear her play on the piano; for she is a mistress of it, who could be a professional if she wished. I then suggested it was time to leave, and Mrs. Bamberger, John, and I thanked Cecil for his hospitality and started back to Cairo.

On our way, as we passed the pyramids Mrs. Bamberger said, "How perfect they must have looked covered with white limestone, each great slab fitting perfectly without cement—better than we can do with all our modern inventions."

"Perhaps we have a good deal to learn from the great civilizations of the past when they were in the zenith of their power and glory and Ra the sun god was worshiped. Why isn't the sun a wonderful embodiment of the great Spirit for those who must have a personal God?"

"Not such a bad idea," quoth John, "but do you see this bridge? Three nights ago a bomb was thrown at six British soldiers, all of whom were wounded, one killed."

"Who did this?" I asked.

"The men who do not want the British and Egyptians to part in peace, who wish the British to leave Egypt at once and entirely, pay young men to drive by in a car and throw the bombs. If the boys—and they are not much more—are caught, it is they who pay with their lives, not the real assassins. The mentally deranged man who tried to assassinate Franklin Roosevelt and killed the Mayor was not the real assassin. Young Booth, who fired the deadly shot at Lincoln, was the tool of men who wanted a free hand to plunder the conquered South; they knew Lincoln meant to pay the South for the freed slaves. President Wilson warned us of the hidden government in the United States—at work then, as it is now. The same men who sold out to Hitler in France and Belgium were ready in America to make their private bargain with him—look! Camels! They have been traveling for weeks through the desert, bringing their goods for sale to Cairo."

And on our right we could see a long line of camels, like gray ghosts of an earlier day, as they noiselessly swayed on in a long, long line.

John arrived promptly at six the next evening. I usually prefer to see anyone of importance alone, because I feel freer to speak my thoughts, with no question or criticism from anyone but the person I am trying to persuade and I can then speak from the heart; but Cecil had sent John and I must do the best I could.

The heat of the day was over when we reached an unpretentious house in Heliopolis. We were ushered into a sitting room with modern French furnishing and with the windows like doors as in France; one needs to have the house thoroughly cooled after the intense heat of the day at this season. John spoke to an Egyptian who came in, and I rose to greet him, thinking it was the Sheik, but it was his secretary. A few minutes later His Excellency came in. I cannot describe his garments because his face was so arresting; but I do remember that he wore the traditional long gown, and a rimless cap on his head with a white cloth wound straight around it. He was a handsome man of perhaps sixty, with graying hair and penetrating dark eyes. He looked noble, and he may have been descended from the prophet Mohammed; I knew that he was spiritually a nobleman. John made the introduction, and we spoke French, which is the diplomatic language still in most of Europe and the Middle East.

"I have come all the way from America to see you, Your Excellency. I have been trying to get to Cairo ever since 1943, but as my mission was not considered of importance to the war I was not allowed to come."

"Please take a seat with me on this ottoman, and we will have some coffee, and you can tell me of this mission of yours."

A servant brought in three tiny cups of thick black coffee. The coffee is very sweet and strong, and as one is offered coffee wherever one goes for visits or for any purchase of any importance it is just as well for the non-coffee-drinkers that the cups are small. I suspected that even this tiny cup meant that I should be wakeful and reading half the night; but little did I know that my wakefulness was to be for another reason.

I told His Excellency of the mission that had brought me to Cairo. "For several years," he answered, "I too have had in mind the possibility of co-operation with other leaders of religion for the sake of the world's peace. To have you bring me the news that some one is at work and active on this idea is reason for hope. I shall be glad to help you as I can."

I thought to myself, "The wise men are still to be found in the East, as in the time of Jesus of Nazareth." Aloud I said, "I did not have an idea of the difficulties I should have to encounter. I have discovered that some of the religious leaders are influenced by politics of the material world, that power—the wishes of the State—come before the State that Allah tries to set up in the hearts and minds of His children."

He smiled. "This is unfortunately true. I have lately had a letter from the chief Rabbi in Palestine, asking me if the Arabs and Jews could not be brought to a more friendly spirit through their common belief in God. I was obliged to

93

refuse him because I should have been accused by my Government and those who hate the Jews of using my position for political purposes."

If this had never been done by any religious leaders of the past the accusation would have had little weight, but again and again in the past religious leaders have feared any one or any move that might weaken their power. Jesus was accused by the Sanhedrin of conspiring to destroy the power of Rome, but it was their own power with their own people that they feared to lose, though Jesus said his kingdom was not of this earth. The Bab was shot one hundred years ago at Tabriz because the religious leaders were jealous of his power over the people, and the Shah was made to believe that the Bab threatened his power. The desire for pelf and power, which pass like melting snow in the sun, still keep our world in the throes of war and evil. The world problem is the individual problem, the conquest of self; that victory is the victory that lifts all mankind.

His Excellency said, "Try to get to the peoples the idea of prayer together as a beginning toward the co-operation of the leaders. Diverse though they are, they can pray together for the good of the world and for the peace they all desire; after the peoples once begin, they must and will demand that their leaders co-operate."

"That is a big order, Your Excellency, for one woman."

"Since you write for a newspaper, send me the articles, and I will have them translated into Arabic and published in Egypt."

"You make me very happy by this offer of help. I shall do as you say."

"Shall we go out into my garden for tea? It is cooler now."

"I love gardens, Your Excellency; I have a rose garden at home. Roses I love especially. I have read of the beautiful rose gardens of Persia, but I do not know much of Egyptian and Arab gardens."

94

"Come and I will show you mine."

So John and I followed him out to his garden of lovely roses and shrubs and other flowers.

"What a restful place to come to after the work of the day!"

"Will you not have some tea? I know that is the drink the British and Americans prefer at this hour."

There was a table laid, with cakes and tea. We sat down, and were offered one plate of cakes after another, each kind more delicious than the last, and all with flavors quite unknown to me. Knowing that food and drink offered to a stranger has a greater significance in the East than in the West, I knew that I must not refuse any of the cakes the Pasha offered me; but there was such an "embarras de richesses" it was hard to accept all. I noticed that John refused every other plate of cakes, saying he was going out to dinner at eight; and our host ate nothing at all. I suspected he was saving up for his dinner; but I must sacrifice my digestion on the altar of my mission. At last I had to decline.

"Your Excellency, I shall be ill if I eat one more of these delectable cakes. You surely would not wish to do that to a friend."

He smiled, and said "No, but I wanted you to taste our cakes; for not even in Paris have you our flavors or way of mixing and baking."

"I am complétement épatée—and you know what that means even if Mr. Brinton doesn't; but I have a question to ask. Where can I get a really good translation of the Koran?"

"There is no very good one, Madame. It is difficult to translate into English; a little less difficult into French, which is a more exact language—the symbolism of Arabic in the Koran, and the feeling and sense, and the metaphysical passages. Even our most erudite mullahs are not sure of the metaphysical meaning of the Prophet and its true interpretation."

95

"I have read a translation by an Englishman, but it was a prejudiced one. We are more prejudiced than Islam, for we do not accept Mohammed as a great prophet, while you do accept Jesus Christ as such. Will you tell me some of the meanings in the metaphysical passages?"

"I will send for an expert, since I am not one."

He ordered the servant in waiting to find the man, who soon came—a very tall man of forty perhaps, to whom we were introduced. He salaamed. I asked him if the joys of heaven as described in the Koran were only sensual joys for the less advanced souls; but John interrupted to say he had a dinner engagement and we must be going. (This is another reason for going unescorted on these important visits.)

"At least let me get an answer from this wise man who has come to instruct us."

His Excellency translated my question, and then translated the reply.

"The sensual joys are for the childish souls who would not understand any others, but the wise . . . given the joy of learning further wisdom from the angels; and those of loving hearts are given the joy of being with their beloved ones and learning with them from the angels."

"Your Excellency, I regret that Mr. Brinton's dinner engagement must call us away, for I should have been overjoyed to stay another hour with you and your learned friend, who could have taught me much that I have long wanted to know. If I were not going to India I should beg for another chance of learning. May I thank you for your offer of help once more and now salaam."

John made his adieus, apologizing for taking me away. His Excellency said to me, "Do not be discouraged if you see no results for a time. What you would do has been for hundreds of years the ideal of the wiser men, but our time is more generally concerned with it than was the past. May Allah give you His peace."

And we went away, I to the Continental and John to his dinner. My dinner began with tomato juice, which I supposed was canned American, but was the raw Egyptian. I spent the night with diarrhea and vomiting, as weak as a newborn child. For three days I took no food and then managed to get on a plane for Alexandria. There I was met by my old friend Justice Jasper Yeates Brinton, who did not realize how ill I still felt, and took a roundabout way to his house to show me some sights. But Geneva, his wife, gave me one look and ordered me to bed, where I stayed ten days, and then went home instead of to India.

CHAPTER 7

TO INDIA

Dr. Ananda K. Coomaraswamy, a philosopher known all over India—and all over the world wherever philosophers are loved and honored—was Fellow for Research in Indian, Persian, and Mohammedan art in the Boston Museum of Fine Arts. His researches embraced philosophy, metaphysics, religion, iconography, Indian literature and arts, Islamic art, music, and the place of art in society. He was the author of many books and a very large range of monographs and pamphlets. A bibliography of his writings has been published by *Ars Islamica*, listing some five hundred published items.

Dr. Coomaraswamy sent me an article to help me in my work for Unity of Spirit, saying, "I thought you might like to read this."

Paths That Lead to the Same Summit

The constant increase of contacts between ourselves, who for the purposes of the present article may be assumed to be Christians, and other peoples who belong to the great non-Christian majority, has made it more than ever before an urgent necessity for us to understand the faiths by which they live. Such an understanding is at the same time intrinsically to be desired, and indispensable for the solution by agreement of the economic and political problems by which the people of the world are at present more divided than united. . . . The modern Christian, who thinks of the world

98

as his parish, is faced with the painful necessity of becoming himself a citizen of the world; he is invited to participate in a symposium and a convivium, not to preside, for there is another who presides unseen, but as one of many guests. . . . It has, too, been proposed that in all the schools and universities of the postwar world stress should be laid on the teaching of the basic principles of the great world religions as a means of promoting international understanding and developing a concept of world-citizenship. . . . All need to realize, with Hesiod, that "when God is our teacher, we come to think alike."

For there are as many of these Hindus and Buddhists whose knowledge of Christianity and of the greatest Christian writers is virtually nil, as there are Christians equally learned, whose knowledge of any other religion but their own is virtually nil, because they have never imagined what it would be like to *live* these other faiths. The greatest of modern Indian saints actually practiced Christian and Islamic disciplines, that is, worshipped Christ and Allah, and found that all led to the same goal. He could speak from experience of the equal validity of all these ways, and feel the same respect for each, while still preferring for himself the one to which his whole being was attuned by nativity, temperament, and training. There are many paths that lead to the summit of one and the same mountain.

Never let us approach another believer to ask him to become "one of *Us*," but approach him with respect as one who is already "one of *His*," who *Is*, and from whose invariable beauty all contingent being depends!

If it had not been for my interest in India, and for the fact that I urged the Boston branch of the Women's International League for Peace and Freedom to invite Madame Pandit to speak, not in a small hall, but in a large one, I should not have met Mrs. Coomaraswamy, and later her husband. She and I tried to make Madame Pandit's speech and contacts memorable. Ambassador William Phillips and Mrs. Phillips, who had known her in India, gave a dinner for her. I also gave one in her hotel, the Ritz Carlton; but when Madame Pandit decided to go to the symphony concert immediately after dessert, it was not exactly a success—except for those who stayed on and had the opportunity of talking to Dr. Coomaraswamy, who gave us what was best of India. Emily Balch, who received the Nobel Peace Prize several years later, thanked me for giving her the opportunity of meeting such a wise man, and they met again at the doctor's house to continue their interchange of thought. I was fortunate to be asked several times to his home, where we discussed Buddhism and Hinduism, of which I knew something through my theosophical studies. We also discussed the work I was doing for Unity in the Spirit. He was interested, and he had written about it better than I could, and knew far more than I did of the work of the wise men of all religions. He undertook to try and prepare me for my journey to India—a preparation that would have meant at least a year's study of history, literature, Hinduism, Buddhism, and Mohammedanism. I knew I must not take that year—for events were moving too fast; the main idea of mankind's fundamental unity must be stressed, and the co-operation of the leaders won, if possible. I explained this to Dr. Coomaraswamy, and he let me go —somewhat reluctantly, for we both knew I was but slightly prepared. I should have to rely on my earnestness, my faith, and the inner help of our Lord. After my return from India I saw him only a few minutes, as his wife wanted to talk to me at the Museum first before we went to his office. I never knew why, for I was anxious to tell him of my experiences in his India, but alas! I never had the chance, because he died of a heart attack soon after. I hope he realized what I had hoped to do, and that my first thought on my return had been for him.

Since 1941, I had dreamed of getting to India. I had badgered any man of importance I could get at to help me to get there in spite of war and the Tory Government. In 1946, when I hoped to go from Egypt to India, since I could probably then get a visa from the Socialist Government of Great Britain, I asked Ambassador Harriman's attaché in London to help me. He asked me if I should still insist on going if the British Government did not want me to go.

"Yes, I shall, since I must get to India in order to accomplish my mission."

"I will get you an appointment with the Under Secretary of State for India, but it may take two or three days."

"Oh, I'll wait. I'm accustomed to waiting. Haven't I waited five years already?"

Three days later I was instructed to go to the India Office near 10 Downing Street at eleven A.M. The India Office was then in a gray stone building. It was late April, but cold as only England can be cold. With the British rugged acceptance of cold, there was no fire in the tiny coal grate fireplace in the waiting room of the Minister's office. I sat down in lonely state to wait the good pleasure of Sir Paul Patrick, and I shivered. I wondered if he had a fire in his office, but when he came and asked me in I saw that he was as fireless as I had been. The office was gloomy, stone-walled, with a desk and two chairs. But Sir Paul was not chilly in his manner. He asked me to sit down, and I noticed that I faced the light. He asked me why I wanted to go to India, and I told him. He asked me whom I hoped to see, and I said Gandhi, any Moslem religious leaders that I could see—Hindus or any others.

"Whom have you seen in the States?"

I told him, and that I had seen the Archbishop of Canterbury, and what his reaction had been.

He turned to his desk and said, "I shall give you an introduction to a Moslem judge in Delhi who is very religious."

Then, with a puckish smile, "You did not expect I would help you, did you? Try and see the Quakers in India; they would help you."

"No, Sir Paul. I did not expect you to help me after my experience with the Tories. Are you Irish?"

"Irish? No, I'm not," rather indignantly.

"But Patrick certainly sounds so. My second cousin was Charles Stuart Parnell, and I'm not ashamed of him."

"My name was French, Patrice de Sainte Patrice, but was anglicized to Patrick."

"I like the French, of course, because of my husband. Now, Patrice de Sainte Patrice, will you turn your face to the light? You have had a chance to inspect me, and it's now my turn."

He laughed and turned to the light. He was not more than forty, with dark hair and eyes—a face with kindness and sympathy in it, and humor.

"Thank you; now I shall know you again—as no doubt you will know me in case I raise ructions in India. Good-bye; and thank you very much indeed." I have not seen him since, but his introduction led to an interesting afternoon in the garden of the Moslem judge in Delhi.

In January, 1947, I decided to start for India. I had my passport from the year before, but I had to get visas for all the countries the TWA plane would touch on my way, first and foremost the British. But with my letter from Sir Paul Patrick I did not expect any trouble, so I boldly engaged my passage and my seat on the plane for four days from then, and then went to the British Consulate in Boston.

"It will take three weeks, Madame, to get a visa from London."

"But I am leaving in four days. Why can't you give me one?"

"The visas for India have to be decided on in London."

"But in London last year the Under Secretary, Sir Paul Patrick, told me I could go. Here is a letter from him, and another from my Under Secretary of State."

"Sorry, Madame, but we have to get our orders from the London office."

"But this is absurd! I just can't wait three weeks."

"You might try the New York office."

"I suppose I'll have to."

So I took a train to New York, and at the British Consulate was told the same story. I insisted something could be done there and then.

"You might try the commercial department downstairs."

Downstairs I went, and talked to a man there.

"We can't do anything for you; but have you tried the top man upstairs? The man in charge can do things when the underlings cannot."

"Thank you; I will try."

The top man was pointed out to me, and I repeated my request for a visa to India.

"We shall have to write to London."

"And it will be three weeks before you get an answer, and I must leave by TWA for India in four days."

"Sit down, won't you? And explain to me why you wish to leave so soon."

I sat down and told him at some length about the mission, my conversation with Sir Paul, and the interest our Secretary of State had shown by his help with our diplomatic officers. I must have spoken earnestly, because he got up and led me to a clerk.

"Give this lady a visa for India now."

I was so surprised I hardly knew how to thank him; but I got my visa. I then went to the Egyptian Consul for a visa, since the plane stopped at Cairo for a night; I had no difficulty because the Consul knew me. That night I spent in New York, and the next day flew to Washington with a

TWA official to get an Arabian visa, since the plane stopped at Dahran. We went at once to the Arabian Minister; but it was within ten minutes of closing time, and would he take five minutes extra for a hurried American? Not he. No pleading of mine or the TWA official would move him; we could come back tomorrow. What is time to an Easterner? The eternal now is of supreme importance, and his now was not to impinge even five minutes on his time for going home.

"There is no use trying to move him," said my TWA friend. "I know from experience. You take a plane home, do your packing, and I will meet you at the Logan Airport in two days, half-an-hour before you take off, with the Arabian visa, which I will get tomorrow."

And so it was done. I spent the night in Boston, and at the airport had my photograph taken by the press, since I was the first woman to fly to India from Boston.

On the plane I met Dr. K. N. Katju, Governor of West Bengal, who was interested in my mission and wanted me to visit him, but I did not succeed in fitting this in.

The plane stopped at Karachi; but we were not allowed to leave the airport, since it was not an official stop, merely for refueling. I had left Boston the end of January, but here it was like summer. Karachi was not then in the Pakistan State, but Mohammed Ali Jinnah had made it his headquarters from which to carry on his fight to divide Moslem and Hindu India.

We flew on to Bombay, and the TWA bus landed us at the Taj Mahal Hotel. The Indian at the desk told me there was no room for me. I showed him my letter from the American Express Company saying I had a room reserved. He looked at it carefully, and then remarked that it was dated two weeks earlier. It was true; and I had failed to take the plane two weeks earlier.

"I have come to India for the first time; I have special work to do; and I must have a room."

"We have nothing but a room in a dormitory."

This was not true, as I found out later; he wanted a bribe to give me a room. But I believed him, and took a quarter of a room with a sagging cot bed. Since the other three women had taken all the room in the two "armoires" and the one bureau, I hung my clothes over a screen before the door. The next morning a small black woman appeared in a white cotton sari and asked to be my ayah or maid. I have never had a personal maid, but because she said her son could find no work because he was a Muslim in a Hindu community, and she had two children, I took her on. She washed my clothes, which for many years I had done myself. She escorted me to the American Consul, Mr. Lamont, protected me crossing the streets from being killed by taxis, told me how much to pay for taxis or anything I bought. She told me she would bring in my morning tea, since the man servant, the "bearer," must not see me undressed. The "old woman" and the two younger women let the "bearer" come in when they were in their slips or nighties. The "old woman" was a peroxide blonde, rather skinny, a German, now American, who talked loud to the "bearer" and ordered my ayah out of the room because "there are too many people in here." My ayah could not forgive her, so she is an "old woman!" I dare say I am as old, but I do not dye my hair.

Mr. Lamont had put me in touch with a Hindu in his office, who told me who were the most holy men of several religions in Bombay. I decided to go first to see Swami Sambuddhananda, who the year before was chairman of a great meeting here of all religions, Christians included, to discuss not their diversities but their unity.

My ayah and I drove out of Bombay twelve miles to see the Swami at his ashrama. These brown- and black-skinned people, men and women, are really handsome. Beauty is not rare, as with us, but everywhere. The girls are lovely in their flowing saris of many different colors. The white-collar men usually wear ugly European clothes, but the laborers wear what looks like a white—sometimes dingy—cloth wrapped around the waist, hanging to the knees rather full, one end drawn from the back between the legs and tucked up and into the cloth around the waist, so their legs look draped to the knee—something like a divided skirt.

We were driving along the sea wall on a wide cement street, passing modernistic apartment houses, schools and playgrounds, bamboo huts with goats and naked and half-naked children running in and out of their entrances, and tiny food stalls in the poor quarters of the villages. We passed several dumps, and in one I saw an almost skeleton creature, naked except for a loin cloth, hunting for food in the rubbish. This is not the famine-stricken region, only one where the poor of India never get enough to eat. I shall never forgive myself for not stopping the car to give to this hungry human being.

At the ashrama or retreat, I was shown the way up an outside flight of stairs to a small room opening on a balcony. My ayah squatted on the balcony while I went in the room. There were two photographs on the wall of Swami Vivekenanda and a colored print of Krishna looking radiant. Swami Sambuddhananda came in clad in saffron. The back of his clean saffron shirt, hanging straight to his knees, was wearing thin. He put his two palms together and touched his forehead with the tips of his fingers, and I did the same. He asked me to sit down, and I explained why I had come. Then he spoke.

"The first need is co-operation among the different religions. If we have that, and the religious leaders will work together, we have a strong foundation. The second need is the co-operation among statesmen and politicians who represent the material desires of the nations, not the spiritual longing. The peoples long for unity and peace; not luxury, but the basic human needs, such as food, shelter, clothing, heat, recreation. But the politicians are often used by the wealthy to further greater power and luxury."

"I know that the swamis I have met in America have been teaching that all religions have the same source, but man being diverse naturally seeks the expression of his diversity in his spiritual life."

"Diversity is the blossoming of the creative urge. Does the rose disdain the lily? A cup of water has different names in every language, but man can quench his thirst with it regardless of its Greek, Latin, German, English, or Sanskrit name. When will man recognize this? He is beginning to know this, for the Kaliyug, the dark age, is passing."

I rose to leave, as the Swami had been called away several times and I had no right to take more of his time. I saluted him in the Indian fashion. Why could not our men and women in important positions who have to meet many people, sometimes several hundred at one time, avoid the exhaustion of shaking hands by adopting the Indian fashion? When I met Mrs. Eisenhower at a Republican reception for her just before the election, I knew she was to shake hands with 500 of the 2,000 women in the Sheraton Plaza ballroom, and I was sorry for her; so when I was introduced I gave her the Indian salute, and said, "I don't want you to get shaker's cramp." She smiled and took both my arms. "I owe you a letter and you will get it," and I did. I hope that India may teach us not to exhaust our leaders by the custom of shaking hands when their strength is so necessary to the good of the state.

The next day I went to see Mr. G. Kapodia, a Jain, in his office, for he was also a businessman. He explained the difference between the Jain and the Hindu belief.

"We do not believe that Nirvana means the loss of the individual soul of its individuality, won after so many, many lives of evolution, or, as we say, reincarnation. The Brahmins teach that the perfected soul is reabsorbed into the ocean of

Brahma as the rivers are lost in the sea. We say that the soul grows to realize its oneness with the All and with each part of the All, but it does not therefore lose its own identity, which should enhance and glorify the All. We also feel that we have no right to take any life except vegetable life.

"I find this interesting, as it appeals to my reason and intuition."

"When you go back to America, dear lady, will you not organize a world meeting of the different religions and call on me to represent the Jains?"

"You are asking for a great effort on my part, when I have not finished the work I am doing now. Try and induce someone else to organize a general religious congress," and I said good-bye.

Not very long after, this letter came from him:

MOTICHAND & DEVIDAS,

Solicitors and Notary Public
Motichand G. Kapadia,
 Tanubhai D. Desai   Bombay, 5th February, 1947
Contesse Dedons de Pierrefeu,
Madam,

I was very glad to talk with you very recently about the fundamentals of Jainism. I may state that Jains believe in Ahimsa (i.e. non-violence), and are very much interested in toleration so far as religion is concerned.

They believe in evolution of the soul, its individuality and progress from stage to stage, and they believe in universal brotherhood, which is not limited to humanity only but extends to animals and even to the vegetable kingdom.

I am very much interested in a movement which may bring about fusion of religions based upon consideration of interesting facts relating to each religion, in a spirit of fairness to the others.

I am glad to note that you are working in the same direction. I wish you good luck.

                              Yours faithfully,
                              Motichand G. Kapadia

I talked to all sorts of people—if they could speak English or French. I sat near a Britisher at lunch and spoke to him, wondering if he would be shocked at a forward American. He was willing to talk, but told me after a bit that he was going to be frank and tell me the British were getting sick of being kicked around by the Americans. So I explained as much as I could about the different elements in a democracy. "You can't expect all Americans to want to make a loan to the British which they know can't be repaid. Many of us know next to nothing of international finance, and we suspect we are not being given the real reason for the loans we make. President Roosevelt has to get the isolationists' approval in Congress before we can act."

"You Americans talk as if you had won the war, but we had to fight alone for a year."

"You think you won the war in that first year. We say that if it had not been for us and our help you never could have won the war. Stalin tells his people that Russia won the war alone. Why not agree that we won it together?"

"Well, I expect we did."

"How do you feel about the division of India that Mohammed Ali Jinnah is trying to bring about?"

"Excellent idea to keep the Hindus and Moslems divided until the Tories come in again, and good old Churchill can get his hands on the Empire once more. The Indians can't rule this great country, they are too easy to bribe."

"Perhaps a subject people is weakened morally and intellectually by its conqueror."

"Nonsense! If you have the guts and the brains, you'll make a chance for freedom."

"What do you think of trying to get the religious leaders of the world to co-operate for world peace?"

"Not a bad idea, if you can get them to, but I don't see much chance of that."

"Well, that's what I'm here for. Wish me luck and good-bye, as I must be going."

"Glad to have met you. I do wish you the best of luck. We Anglo-Saxons must stick together."

That afternoon I spent nearly an hour with the Director of Tata Airways, Sir Homi Midi, a Parsi or Zoroastrian. The Parsis have kept out of politics and have done well in business, and this has made other groups jealous of them. I had read that morning a Parsi article in the paper urging Parsis to take part in India's efforts for freedom, and not stand aloof as though they were not true Indians.

The Parsis, originally from Persia, did not probably mix much at first with the Hindus and Moslems, due to their religion, just as the Aryan Hindus did not mix with the Dravidian race they conquered when they overran India. The Dravidians were black but not Negroid, but as they became the subject race through conquest they were relegated to the menial tasks, and the Brahmin priesthood forbade intermarriage. As in America, there was nevertheless admixture of the dark and light races; and I was told that the Dravidians were hardy and many were brilliant mentally. The streams of the human races meet and mingle till one day there may be but one race—the human.

Sir Homi, with the Persian coloring, was a handsome man of middle age, very gracious to this American with a dream of world unity.

Sir Homi asked me about America, and what we thought of the Labor Party's promise to free India.

"Most people believe it is necessary, and feel that it is due to Ghandhi's peaceful non-co-operation policy. He is a great soul, who has given the world an example every country should follow."

"Yes, all the poor people in India of all faiths love him; but there are members of the strictest Hindu faith who think he is too liberal and is teaching too many changes, especially his stand for Untouchables."

"We also have our difficulties with those who want the Negro kept in his place, as they put it, but slowly the Negro is coming into his own; and Stalin is helping by his propaganda on our lynchings and cruelty. Funny, coming from Stalin. Nevertheless we are being forced to face facts, and realize that we must give our American Negroes and our American Indians the same chance as any other citizens. But I must leave you."

"Stay as long as you can, as it is not every day that I have the privilege of a visit from an outstanding lady from America."

"Thank you, Sir Homi. I wonder if you would give me a letter which would help me to get a passage on your airline? I want to move quickly in India, because the heat is beginning and I find it affects my health." So he gave me a letter which would be honored by the Tata Airways, and I then made my adieus, with many thanks for Sir Homi's courtesy.

The Hotel Taj Mahal was a handsome building with every modern convenience (except for the women's dormitory), and high-ceilinged rooms that made for coolness. The hotel was on the wide, paved road that curved along the sea. To the left as one looked out to sea was the Gate to India, Oriental arches like the Arc de Triomphe in Paris, but not as high and with no statues. Here the sauntering people gathered while sailboats loaded and unloaded their cargo and passengers, at the stone steps that went down into the water. How did this Oriental city differ from the West? The rhythm was unhurried; the streets were filled with men in white—tight white trousers, with knee-length, divided-skirt effect; white robes, some gray with dust; a few men in khaki shorts; and the dragomen in long robes of bright colors with a long coat of another bright shade; the women in bright-colored saris, or poorer women in just a white cotton with some bright border; Moslem women in black gowns with their faces covered. Some white women in Western dress, and a few darker skinned as well. There were few beggars; but the very poor lay here and there on the sidewalks in nothing but a dark cloth to the knees, dark with dirt. Children up to three and four years were carried by men and women straddled on the hip. I saw little tots in their father's arms dressed in brilliant-colored satin or velvet, with bangles on their little arms, earrings, and their eyes darkened with kohl. The people usually had serene faces, but some of the young men scowled at a Westerner. Perhaps our one-time ally Stalin had something to do with hate—a passion so destructive to the hater. But here, as everywhere, a friendly smile smoothed the way.

Our Consul, Mr. Lamont, got me an interview with a prominent automobile manufacturer, Sultan Chinoy, Bombay Garage, head of the automobile industry in India. Since I was listed on my passport as going to India on business for the New Hampshire Ball Bearings Company, I felt it my duty to do what business I could. We talked ball bearings for some time; but, since he knew little of the manufacturing and technical end, he called in his British manager to talk to me. The manager was not interested in precision ball bearings, but said he needed larger ball bearings for use in automobiles. After the manager left, Sultan Chinoy said to me,

"I have many English and American friends, but I see no way of avoiding a blood bath, which might come in days, weeks, or months; and when it comes everyone with a white skin will be slaughtered. The people will take anyone who is white for British, whether they be American, French, German, or any other white race."

I confess this frightened me; but I went on to speak of my desire to see Ali Mohammed Jinnah, who wanted to divide India.

"I know him well, since my father gave him his education. He was born a Hindu, but changed his religion and became a follower of the prophet Mohammed. He is an ambitious man. Why do you wish to see him?"

"I do not think India should be divided, for that would make her weaker; and she will need all her strength to give her people wise government—as wise as the Emperor Akbar, who tried to unite the Muslins and Hindus. He was friendly to the Hindus and invited the wise Hindus to expound their religion to him. There were no famines, as in the last 200 years."

"So you know of our wise Emperor? Would we had such a man now, for the Hindus and Moslems hate each other."

"They would not hate if they listened to Gandhi. This has been an enlightening talk. I certainly hope you are wrong about a blood bath. Good-bye, Sultan Chinoy."

"Good-bye, my dear Countess. It has been interesting to meet someone who appreciates our great Akbar."

I was worried about this talk of a blood bath; so I went to Mr. Lamont and told him what I had heard.

"Do you believe this, Mr. Lamont?"

"I do. I am prepared to leave here with my wife at any moment."

"Heavens! Do you think I should leave?"

"You must decide that yourself. It may not come for some time."

Should I go home or stay? I did not look forward to being slaughtered by infuriated Indians; yet I had come for a purpose and should go on with it. We must all die sometime; when better than doing one's duty? I decided to stay, and hoped there would be no blood bath. As we know, the blood bath came, but it was not the British they killed, but each other—Hindus and Moslems; and for this the British Government was responsible, as any government is responsible that governs by the Roman axiom "divide and rule." A friend of mine in Hancock, New Hampshire, had told me before I started for India that fifty years before he was on the Mediterranean in a ship from India, where he met a British officer and they became friendly. He said to this officer one day,

"Is it true that it is the policy of the British Government to send out agents to stir up trouble between the Hindus and the Moslems?"

"Yes, I ought to know, for I am one of them."

Great Britain was of course not to be blamed any more than any other country that tries to hold its possessions. Government leaders know their people will blame them if they fail to hold what the Government has acquired, especially those who have a direct interest in the financial returns from a conquered country. There is not a country in the world probably that has not at some time used the axiom of "divide and rule." Great Britain has been losing her conquered territories, and the wise souls of the country must thank God that this is so. We of the United States of America will be able to thank God when we have given back to the Indians and the Negroes the same chances for self-development that others have in this melting-pot of humanity; and when we make it our dream to help any country that is in need—not by careless gifts or loans of money, but as the Friends do, by sending groups abroad to live among the people and show them how to develop and irrigate their land, how to make the tools they need, how to make friends, how to forget their differences of faith, of custom, of possessions.

Two places I longed to see that were not in my itinerary —the Himalaya Mountains, and Agra and the Taj Mahal. I decided to go to Agra first. I asked the American Express Company to engage a room for me at a hotel in Agra, and to get my tickets and berth on the train. As I spoke no Hindustani, I also asked to be escorted to the train by one of their agents. As I was leaving one Sunday evening, the agent, who wanted his Sunday, seemed to think I ought to be able to find the right train, my compartment, and berth without his help; but I, to his obvious disgust, still insisted I needed his help. We reached my car half an hour early, and to my amazement found my compartment filled with men, women, and children.

"Good gracious! are all these people going in this compartment?"

"No, not all. Good evening, Madame." And off he went.

The compartment was not like ours, nor like the British. There were four wooden berths, in pairs, one above the other; no mattresses or bedclothes—which was why every traveler took his bed with him, a very thin mattress that could be rolled up like a steamer rug with a strap around it. There was a large space—or was later, when the Indian travelers' many friends and relatives left; two wicker armchairs; and beyond the chairs two toilets for men and women. I was able to find part of a seat, and watched the men, women, and children all talking, and wished I knew the language. In about twenty minutes some of these people began to leave, saying farewell to two men and a woman who were sitting on a lower berth. Presently, to my great relief, everyone had gone but the two men and the lady—we were not going to travel *en masse*. The younger of the two men asked me which berth I had, and I showed him my ticket, and found I had one of the upper berths. He offered to take the upper and let me have his lower, but I thanked him and said I could manage the upper well enough. The ice was broken—though really there was no ice in India to break; at any rate I never found any.

"Where are you going?"

"To Agra, to see your beautiful Taj Mahal. At what time do we get there?"

"At seven tomorrow morning."

"Do you go as far as Agra?"

"No, we all leave the train at midnight."

"I wonder how I shall know when we get to Agra?"

"I will tell the boy who waits on this car to let you know."

"Oh! That would be kind, as I speak no Hindustani. Where did you learn to speak English as the Americans do?"

"In America, where I have studied. I am a lawyer, and I hope to go back there."

"I should like to meet your wife."

He asked my name and then introduced us. She understood English, but did not speak as fluently as he did. Naturally they asked me why I had come to India, and I told them. People are usually interested in what seems a hopeless mission, I suppose, because they think it must take a certain crazy courage.

"But why do you go to Agra?"

"Just to see your Taj Mahal by moonlight, if possible."

"Ah, it is beautiful, and much loved, one of the beauties of the world; but America is beautiful outside of her cities."

"Have you seen Washington, D. C.?"

"No, not yet."

"Washington is our most beautiful city. I do not like cities; I like the country. But Washington has wide streets and many trees, some very handsome buildings, and the Lincoln Memorial. Try and see that if nothing else, for it has also near it the lovely cherry trees given us by Yukio Osaki, one-time mayor of Tokyo, the man who did his best for a more democratic Japan. I met his wife through Mrs. Thomas

Perry, whose husband has taught in the University of Tokyo. One of Yukio Osaki's daughters spent a weekend at my home, at the same time as Jujun Saito of the well-known Saito family of Japan, who was then at Harvard. He afterward gave me two beautiful pale green vases inlaid with silver dragons. He told me it was the first time he had been invited to an American home."

"I must see Washington the next time I go to America. Have you seen much of Bombay?"

"No, very little; but what I have seen I like—especially the Gate to India."

"When you come back, let us know. We should like to show you Bombay."

But when I came back I was too weak from the heat, so I never was shown Bombay by these kind people, who gave the boy porter such careful instructions on helping me in any way he could.

I decided to unfasten my bedroll and try sleeping in my upper berth, which I did fairly comfortably. When I woke at dawn my Indian friends had left, the train had stopped at some station, and I watched the Hindus who had got out to make their prescribed ablutions, each with a pot of water. They were rinsing their noses, mouths, and eyes, an ancient and healthy protection against disease. We should do well to imitate them.

The boy porter saw me off at Agra with my suitcases, and even put me into a taxi, for which he was rewarded as though he had been an American. I was taken to a small, very good hotel in a garden, with cool, high-ceilinged rooms, simply but well furnished. After the dusty, rather flat and arid country the train had been through, the trees and garden were delightful.

At lunch I met a man and his wife from Warner, N. H. He was a big-game hunter, and his wife did some shooting with him. There was also an American correspondent from China who was worried about an American woman she knew in China, who was very poor and needed help. That afternoon I went to see the Taj Mahal with my New Hampshire acquaintances; therefore I missed its moonlit mystery.

India's most famous monument 300 years ago took the Emperor Shah Jahan twenty-two years to build, and cost $6,200,000, as an imperial mausoleum to hold the body of his favorite queen, Mumtaz Mahal. She died after giving birth to her fourteenth baby in fourteen years. Most people have seen pictures of this mausoleum; but to get the feeling of this snow-white tomb, this palace of the dead, one must see it on the spot. You enter through a two-story red stone gateway, rather like the Gate to India in Bombay, but far more imposing. When you are through these great gates you see the white Taj Mahal before you, but beyond a stretch of clear water—in a marble tank paralleled with cedars. This long stretch of limpid water mirrors curving white marble steps that lead to the terrace, and the great doorway. The Lincoln Memorial in Washington has a similar mirror stretch of water, between it at one end and the Washington Monument at the other. Lincoln's tomb, however, is a part of our capital city, while Queen Mumtaz Mahal's is set apart in its own park and garden, among flowering shrubs and rare trees. With the eyes of the soul I saw flowering fruit trees on either side of the long pool instead of the cedars that are now there. I asked the guardian of the gate—he told me there used to be fruit trees but the Viceroy had put in the cedars. I went inside and saw the screen around the cenotaph of the Emperor and his beloved Mumtaz—which was an arabesque mosaic of twelve kinds of semiprecious and precious stones of surpassing beauty. The beauty of the Emperor's dream and the architect's realization of that dream is still there in testimony of a great and enduring love that will never die, even though the tomb may sometime disappear.

"Yes, but in our climate certain plants need a great deal of water."

"I can understand that."

Her husband came back and joined us.

"We were talking of gardens."

"Yes, my wife leads me around her garden to show me her improvements, but I know nothing about flowers."

As soon as he came back she subsided, and he took over the conversation. I told him why I had come to India. He went into the house and brought out a speech he had delivered to young Muslims at one of their universities. It was on religion, especially their own. I confess I was taken aback at being asked to read it aloud to him, but I now see his reason. He would be sure I had read it, that I had read it slowly, and that he could discuss it point by point. I only wondered if his wife were interested. It was pithy and well-reasoned; was he not a judge? I exclaimed at the points he made, and then he evaluated them. I found that he knew as much about the Christian religion as I did. He made the point that if a religion did not produce great men of spiritual stature it was no longer of any value, and the truth must be looked for elsewhere. When it grew cool we went into the house, and I let my mind descend to lower things—my taxi meter for one. He read from a book of his which was about to appear. His wife excused herself, since it was the time for prayer. I tried to excuse myself, but he had not finished what he wanted me to hear.

"What about your prayers?" I asked.

"It is not quite time for mine. I hope you will come and visit us next month at our home in the north. I want you to meet some of our Moslems, who are as deeply interested as you are in spiritual truths."

"This is very kind of you. I should be delighted, if I am still in India; but I am sure I am keeping you from your prayers."

On that we parted. He put me in my taxi, and said in farewell, "I shall be going to a meeting of the Moslem League in a few weeks, and I shall ask the Moslems to co-operate with the congress."

I have often wondered if he remembered to do this; and, if so, what the other members of the League answered.

The next morning my American hunter friends from Warner took me with them to buy some ivory in Delhi—the old city, with crowded, narrow streets; the dogcarts and taxis had to move slowly because of the people of all ages— and the holy cows. The cows know they are holy and take full advantage of it; they wander along the streets, stopping when they feel like it, helping themselves from the little open stalls and shops to any food that a cow would enjoy, or lying down in the street for a rest. I put out my hand to stroke a young bossy near me, for I like animals even if they are holy. Our taxi man seized my arm. "Do not touch it, Madame, or we might start a riot. No one dares touch a holy cow, and they are all holy."

"But I wasn't going to hurt it. I like cows, and that is such a pretty young one."

"Madame does not know the custom of the country. The Hindus might tear you to pieces."

"Then you are a Moslem. Don't worry, I won't touch."

I followed my friends up a narrow little stair to a small room, where three or four men sat crosslegged carving ivory. The proprietor came forward and showed us various carved ivory ornaments, elephants, tigers, carved tusks, ivory combs; and I bought several ivory necklaces of graduated, carved elephants strung with a bead between, and a larger elephant as a pendant. They were not expensive, considering the work involved; but I suppose the carvers earned only a bare living. They say that it is lucky only if the elephants are trumpeting; but my necklaces all have hanging trunks, alas!

Two days later I took a plane to Karachi for my appointment with Mohammed Ali Jinnah. I found the hotel very cool and comfortable, with a garden; garden and hotel were enclosed. My appointment was for four o'clock at the Nawab of Bhopal's palace. I hired a carriage with a driver who could speak English. As usual, I was ahead of time; so we had to drive round and round the walls of the palace. The Nawab's summer residence turned out to be more like a roomy Mediterranean villa. The Nawab had lent it to Mohammed Ali Jinnah, President of the Moslem League. There he lived with his sister, and from there conducted his campaign for the division of India into Moslem and Hindu states. I was going to try and dissuade him; but Dr. Ananada Coomaraswamy had told me at his home in Needham before I left for India that it was Jinnah's sister who was the moving spirit behind the whole movement; she had great influence over her brother. It was she who met me as I left my carriage outside the gate and came to the entrance of the palace. She was tall, handsome and slender, with iron-gray hair, fine, large, dark eyes. She spoke perfect English, as she and her brother had lived long in London.

"Will you sit in the garden with me? My brother has a visitor. It is Harold Macmillan," she said, with a gleam in her eyes; "he has been with my brother for two hours"—another gleam. The name struck a chord in my memory; but it was not till the next day that I remembered in what connection I had heard the name. He was a Tory, a man well known in Conservative circles, a Churchill man. What was he doing here, since in August the Labor Government had agreed to give India back to the Indians? Did Churchill still hope to keep a hold on India?

I made a tentative remark about hoping India would not be divided.

"Why should it not be divided for the good of the Moslems? Have we not as much right as the Hindus to control our destiny? Why should they govern us, when we abhor their religion and their holy cows, that are allowed to eat anyone's crops or the produce in our city shops?"

"Of course these customs must be very annoying; but is there not some way of coming to an understanding about them in regard to public places and the property of others?"

"You do not seem to understand that we are in the minority."

"Yes, I know that. But from my study of history I have seemed to learn that it is the minority, if it is a wise minority, that by persistence can change unjust laws."

"You do not know India or the Hindus."

"I think I know something of human nature, and something of what Gandhi has accomplished for India. Has he not freed her?"

"Oh, Gandhi! You Americans think only of Gandhi. My brother could have done as much for India; and he will do more for us Moslems, when we have the State of Pakistan."

The sun had gone down, and it was getting cold in the garden. I wished I had brought my coat, but I had not expected to have to wait so long. Also I was tired of arguing with Miss Jinnah. I remembered what Dr. Coomaraswamy had told me of her, and I realized he was right. I changed the conversation to the weather, to my hotel's convenience, and to the city of Karachi, until Mr. Jinnah appeared at the door with Harold Macmillan, a rosy-cheeked Briton. They shook hands; Macmillan went out to his car; and Mr. Jinnah came to meet me. I had the feeling that he was too important to be bothered by an unimportant person like a correspondent; but he was very cordial, and apologized for keeping me waiting —"but the business was important." He led me into the

a year ago, and he offered to translate anything I might write on this subject and have it published in Egypt."

"I of course know of Sheik Abd-el-Razek Pasha, but I have never met him. What can I do to help you?"

"Will you spread abroad the need for spiritual co-operation and good will amongst Moslems and Hindus and all other faiths?" As Ali Shah translated, I noticed that the students sitting crosslegged on the floor had stopped their work to listen to the interpreter and their Sufi Master. I continued, "Not only for the sake of all peoples but for the sake of India, who must have unity to develop and take her place among the nations."

The Sufi then replied that he would speak in the mosque on the next great holy day, and would write an article for the newspapers. Would I not give him a photograph of myself to publish with it?

"How good of you to give all this help! I have only a passport photograph with me."

"That will do. Sometimes I can look into the future, and I have seen India and America leading humanity together through the power of the Spirit."

He gave me a pamphlet he had written about imaginary interviews between Edward the Eighth and the Archbishop of Canterbury, with Wallis Warfield Simpson and the king's valet. I read this when I got back to the hotel, and was interested to find that his reaction to the abdication had been much like mine—concerned with the Prince's desire for love and companionship. Other kings of England had taken the wives they loved, regardless of their rank; and Elizabeth Tudor was one result.

The Sufi then gave me a yellow silk handkerchief, put it on my head, and blessed me. He asked me to walk over through the court to his house to meet his wife. I was very glad to go; but we had to leave Ali Shah behind, since he must not look on the Sufi's wife unveiled. I followed the Sufi between walls to another courtyard, and up some steps onto a veranda. There the Sufi motioned me to wait; and in a few moments he came out with a lovely young creature with the eyes of a gazelle, who told me in halting English that her mother was asleep so she had come to welcome me instead. A small boy who looked at me with wide-eyed curiosity was a grandchild. I did not stay long, since there was no Ali Shah to interpret for us; so I made my adieus, and the Sufi and I rejoined Ali Shah and walked to the car together, where I again thanked the Sufi for his promised help. Ali Shah then told me that the yellow square of silk the wise Sufi had given me would bring me blessings and good fortune.

After we had started back in the car, I told Ali Shah how lovely a sight he had missed in not seeing the good Sufi's daughter. He smiled but made no comment—that would not have been good manners.

The Indians are a beautiful people. Nowhere in my travels have I seen so much dignity and beauty. What will they not teach the West, once they have become united as they were under the great Mogul Emperor Akbar? But Jinnah accomplished his dream of separating Hindus and Moslems in the two territories of Pakistan, which are still further separated by Indian territory, with the ensuing horror and bloodshed the world was to see in pictures and read of in its press. Sultan Chinoy had been right about a blood bath, but he had not told me that it would be Indian against Indian. Perhaps he really believed it would be Indian against white.

Dr. N. Purushottam, whom I met through Mrs. Coomaraswamy, very kindly gave me several introductions, but the only one I used was in New Delhi; the others were in other states. It was to his brother-in-law, S. Subramaniam, M.A., Statistician to the Cabinet Secretariat, Government of India, New Delhi, whom I went to see at the Secretariat. After some difficulty in finding his office, I met him—a tall, youngish

Indian who spoke English perfectly. He was very kind; and since I came from his brother-in-law was interested to hear of him. He showed me around the offices of his part of the building, and then said, "I think it might interest you to go to the home of a middle class Indian family. Could you come to my house tomorrow for coffee at five o'clock?"

"I should be delighted. I hope I shall meet your wife. Have you children?"

"I have four."

"Oh! that will be a pleasure. Please tell me how to get to your house."

"I live not far from here in a Government house. Why not take the bus from Delhi, since it stops near my house, and I will meet the bus." So he wrote down the address; and we parted to meet next day at the bus.

On the bus I talked to a young English girl, who was all agog to find I was an American; who wanted to come to America so much that her family later asked me to a picnic which was an orgy of pigeon-shooting that took all my self-control to live through.

Mr. Subramaniam met me at the bus, and we walked to his flat-roof house of cream-colored, plain cement, much like one-story houses in California without the colors. We spoke of India's future, now that she was so soon to be a free country. He was full of hope and plans, as were all the young Indians I talked to. This gave me the feeling that youth would succeed in giving the very poor of India the knowledge and training and freedom from debt that they must have. Most of the men who dreamed and planned and fought for our freedom from England had been young men.

In the central courtyard I saw a tall, oldish man holding a year-old child. Mr. Subramaniam spoke to him, and he stopped in his slow walk and I was able to look at the child.

"This is my youngest, a boy. He is not happy, as he is getting teeth."

133

"Poor dear! You have three others?"

"Yes. The two eldest are girls, and we have another boy."

He spoke in Hindustani to a beautiful girl of about eight who was standing some distance from us. She seemed very shy, so we went to her and I was introduced, but the child made little response.

"It is because of her hand that she is shy of strangers." I then noticed that she could not straighten two of the fingers of one hand.

"Her uncle, Dr. Purushottam, is going to see what can be done for her. Ah! here is my wife. She speaks little English." A pretty little woman had come from a door. She seemed very shy, too, and the language was also a barrier. I saluted her by touching my forehead with my hands together, and she did the same. Then a boy of seven and a girl of nine came out into the courtyard. They spoke English because they went to an English school, and they were delighted to see the lady from America. Mr. Subramaniam asked his wife to get the coffee, and we went into a small sitting room, simply furnished, with a statuette of the goddess Vishnu on the mantel. The goddess had a wreath of fresh flowers around her neck. I think there were three chairs in the room. I was given the most comfortable one, and the two children stood near me. Mrs. Subramaniam was short, with her black hair parted in the middle and done in a low knot on the neck. She had a gentle, quiet face, and smiled shyly at me as her husband told me the names of the girls and their younger brothers. The children were clustered about us. As I love children, we soon were on friendly terms. I told them about my grandchildren, and asked them what they were learning in school. Mrs. Subramaniam came in with the coffee and three cups and he poured it. I took some, though it keeps me awake and gives me a headache the next day. I asked Mrs. Subramaniam where she bought her sari.

"No, my husband buy saris."

"Does he always choose your saris?"

"Yes, I always buy her saris," he said.

"Show us your saris," he said to his wife.

The little wife seemed pleased to get them. They were very bright satins, rather like a man's choice; but she seemed delighted to show them to me, and we both admired them. The sari is very simple to fold—just five yards of material with a border. On the finest gauze saris the border may be eight inches wide in real gold or silver thread, which in case of need can be sold by the weight of the precious metal. It hangs in beautiful lines and folds, very Greek in its look. The eldest daughter brought me a pair of her gold earrings to admire. I decided then that her sister and older brother must have something from me when I could find what I wanted.

Later I said, "I believe you, Mr. Subramaniam, are the fairest and most unprejudiced Indian I have met."

He laughed. "Because I can see both sides I am not popular with either."

"You should have been a judge. Keep your just and fair outlook, even though you should be ground to powder between the left and right." Such men as he will be India's salvation.

I told the children about my family; and the boy told me what he was studying at school. Most English and Americans have to be dumb in the countries we visit, because we do not learn other languages. All too soon it was time for me to leave this happy and devoted family. I said good-bye to each, not forgetting the beautiful, shy little girl who had stayed in the courtyard. Sometime I hope to see them all again.

Mr. Subramaniam had arranged for me to see Prime Minister Jawaharlal Nehru the next day at the Congress building. Mr. Nehru was in his office, and seemed either very tired or very uninterested in a woman from America. I could give him the benefit of the doubt, since he had only lately heard that the British Government was handing India back to the Congress two months earlier than had at first been agreed on, which meant a great amount of preparation. I felt that the less I said to this apparently weary man the easier for him, so I only asked him about the story Mr. Jinnah had told me about Gandhi's going back on the treaty he had signed with Jinnah.

"It was not of much importance, and was merely a mistake in the wording of the treaty. I have seen Mr. Jinnah a good many times to discuss problems of Hindus and Moslems."

I could not help comparing Nehru's lassitude and indifference with Jinnah's eagerness. I left, hoping he would find rest, for he would need it.

I knew from Gandhi's postcard to me that he was with me in spirit on my mission. I knew he would be with me in my attempt, however futile, to convince Ali Mohammed Jinnah that it was not for the good of India or her people that she be divided. Did we not have in America men and women of all religions who lived in peace with each other, even though they now and then were in bitter verbal disagreement? I wanted to meet Gandhi face to face; so I had asked Mr. Subramaniam how to do this.

"Gandhi is walking from village to village begging the Hindus and Moslems to live in peace with each other. We never know what village he has reached till he starts for the next. You would have to have an Indian go with you, and you would have to walk part of the way as you got near him."

"Could you find me someone?"

"I will send a young man to your hotel tomorrow."

"So many thanks."

Meanwhile the weather had been getting hotter and hotter, and I was feeling less and less energetic. The next day I had a slight attack of dysentary; but I talked to the young Hindu Mr. Subramaniam had sent about the trip, and told him I would let him know if I felt able to take it. The next day

I was no better; and remembering how long I had been ill in Cairo and Alexandria with this same illness the year before, I reluctantly decided I had better get home as soon as possible to our food and climate. Two days later I was able to get a plane to Bombay, where I spent one night; and then, after some telephoning about getting out of India without the usual shots in the arm, took a TWA plane home. Dr. Roy knew I was basically in good health.

The following poems were written in love and admiration of a great soul, called Mahatma Gandhi by those who love him, though he himself said he was not one of the Mahatmas —those leaders who guide humanity from the Himalayas and other lonely places removed from the murk of our so-called civilization. If Gandhi was right in saying he was not a Mahatma, he surely is one now. Has he not given his life for his friends, as Jesus did? Did he not forgive his murderers as Jesus did? Did he not call on "Ram! Ram!" with his last breath as Jesus called on His Father? Must man's greatest gift to his fellow men still be his life given in agony, before he can become more than man, truly a Son of God?

Gandhi's March to the Sea

We are marching, we are marching,
Sixty-seven we are marching,
To the salt pans of the sea,
To the free and open sea.
India's soul is moving with us,
Marching millions moving with us.
India's soul is calling, calling.
"I am marching to the sea;
Come with joy and quietly
For I march eternally.
You will have to follow me,
Inchoate although you be.

I lead you love's way
To a sweet and dancing day.
Black and brown men, yellow, white,
You are all a part of me.
I am calling, you must follow
On the March to open sea,
To the salt pans of the sea."

Elsa Tudor
—from Stri Dharma, 1932

Gandhiji

O shining soul!
Within a thin brown body,
Holding an empire
In your weaving hands.
The lion's roars,
The lion's claws,
Leave you unshaken.
We are driven,
We are driven
By the winds of desire,
But you sit quiet in prison,
In the prison we made for you;
Weaving, weaving,
Dreaming, dreaming,
Praying, praying,
Loving, loving,
Fasting to death for us;
We who are torn from the Tree,
Shriveled and hopeless,
Dying the death,
One by one,
Two by two,
Multitudinous
We are driven back to you,

O Gandhiji!
For you are the sap of life.
O shining soul!
Within a thin brown body,
That hold a world
In your patient hands.

> Elsa Tudor
> June, 1933
> *The Modern Review*
> Calcutta, India

These two letters from Ali Shah were sent to certain key people in May, 1950, with the following covering letter:

The enclosed letters speak for themselves.

I beg of you as you believe in God, and as you love your fellow men, to do all in your power to work with Professor Ali Shah in order that the Moslems of the world will know we are their brothers and stand ready with them to resist evil, as our Lord resisted evil, as the prophets of all time have resisted evil. For a long while I have believed that America, in spite of her past sins, must be the country to wrestle with the great evil of atheism, and with those who corrupt the souls of men.

THE MOSLEM UNION

(Devoted to the protection and encouragement of the moral and material well-being of Moslems, and to furthering the spirit of equality between one man and another, as the one essential for a lasting world peace.)

79 Avenue des Champs Elysees, Paris

18th May, 1950

Dear Madam:
My friend Lord Sinha has handed over to me a letter, which you kindly wrote to him from London after reading his letter

in *The Times* of 1st of May 1950 regarding the Moslem Union. I write as the President of the Union, and to tell you that we would greatly welcome your co-operation in regard to a Moslem–Christian rapprochement in order to face and to fight the evil of materialism and godlessness which is crawling up to us not only in Asia, but working so rapidly on toward Europe, and might reach the United States sooner than most people believe. The Union is in essence an organization whose members are all Moslems; and the first purpose of the movement is to bring about a closer unity amongst us, and then to pull our weight in making a common cause with the Christian world for a fight for God. That which the Sheik of Al Azhar told you in Cairo was very true, but the spirit of unity has now come into the hearts of rank and file of all Moslems— Moslems as people—and we are working here by holding conferences, publishing booklets, and using other usual publicity methods to make our purpose known to the world. It is my desire to come to the United States one day soon to seek co-operation with those Christians who may be inclined to stretch their hand of friendship to us in this work of God: a work which, you so justly remark, is most urgent now and not ten or fifteen years hence. The danger is upon us all now, and we must do all we can to call forth all forces of good to act against evil. Moslem kings have written to me signifying their active support of the movement, and even humble peasants of Arabia and Persia and elsewhere have shown the same interest. Will you be so kind as to write to me at my London Club? The address is typed above. Tell me what you and your friends in America can do to help us, and help us soon, in our quest to make a common cause with the Christians at large. I am most anxiously awaiting your early reply; and meantime, dear Countess, accept my assurances of esteem.

Yours sincerely,
Professor Syed Ikbal Ali Shah

THE MOSLEM UNION

27th May, 1950

Madam:

Thank you very much for your kind letter dated the 22nd instant, in which you say that you are about to interest various religious groups in the United States in regard to our ALL WORLD MOSLEM endeavour to produce unity amongst mankind for a brotherly world. In England, unfortunately, I find that the organised Church as such is too much divided amongst itself and too much concerned in its local troubles, to think enough about matters beyond that which happens in Piccadilly or Tooting. The people here produce practically no reaction; they are either in a coma, or something has robbed them of that extensive vision that they once possessed; therefore, their "spiritual awakening," like any other awakening, must come to them from America. I have thus lost all hopes of their sitting up and doing something to stem the tide of godless materialism that has already overcome half of South-east Asia. Will you be so good as to do all that you can possibly do to get things moving in America towards a unity with the Moslem world, so that we can fight materialism—for it is not too late, even now. The only people who have so far come to listen to our exhortations are the Roman Catholics, but not the English Roman Catholics; and an enclosed article of mine might be of interest to you and your friends. But we as Moslems do not want to get mixed up with the Roman Catholic and Protestant schools of Christians and their struggle against each other, so as to be stigmatized as being helped only by Catholics, and the other group keep away from us on that score. Next week I am invited to go to Paris to attend a conference of WORLD ORGANISATION FOR BROTHERHOOD which an American movement is holding there, and its vice-president came to see me at my London Club. On the 12th June, 1950, we are holding our own World Moslem

Conference in England, and that might be a "news peg" for the Voice of America broadcasting. I am not sure as to what the United Nations might be able to do in this connection, for if that organisation had given one-tenth of its attention to spiritual values as compared to purely materialistic wrangling of nations things would be much closer to peace than they are today. The church leaders in Boston, whom you hope to meet, I trust are different from the clergy here, for here they consider me to have no hopes at all till I embrace Christianity. I think that a real effort can be made rather by the lay Christian than the hide-bound professional preacher towards this coming together; and I am certain that pious people like your good self will do more than many church dignitaries (at least that is my impression of them in England). I look forward to hearing from you prior to my going to Egypt for another Moslem World Conference at a very early date. Please address your reply to me personally here in London, so that I may attend to it myself, rather than sending your reply to Paris. My address is the National Liberal Club, Whitehall Place, London, S.W. (I).

Yours sincerely,
Professor Syed Ikbal Ali Shah
(President of the Moslem Union)

The following article appeared in the *Boston Daily Globe* on September 29, 1951, under the heading, "President Urges Churches United Against Communism."

President Truman called on the churches of the world tonight to unite in a "common affirmation of faith" against the evils of Communism and said he regretted that so far he has been unable to get Christian leaders to work toward that goal.

Warning that "the whole human enterprise" and the very future of the Word of God" is in danger.

Mr. Truman said that such an affirmation "would testify to the strength of our common faith and our confidence in its ultimate victory over the forces that oppose it."

The President spoke before the Washington Pilgrimage of American Churchmen meeting at the National City Christian Church.

He reminded the religious leaders that the authors of the Declaration and the founders of the Republic have handed down a religious heritage which "imposes great obligations upon us."

Mr. Truman said he had been trying for "some time" to bring a number of the great religious leaders of the world together, "in a common affirmation of faith and a common supplication to the one God that all profess."

"I have asked them to join in one common act which will affirm these religious and moral principles on which we all agree."

"I am sorry to say that it has not yet been possible to bring the religious faiths together for this purpose of bearing witness that God is the way of truth and peace."

"Even the Christian churches have not yet found themselves able to say with one voice, that Christ is their Master and Redeemer and the source of their strength against the hosts of irreligion and the danger of a world catastrophe."

Mr. Truman said despite the barriers that divide the different churches "there is common bond of brotherhood that underlies them all."

"God grant that we may speak together as brothers of His power and His mercy, and bear witness of Him against those who deny Him," he said solemnly. "May God unite the churches, and bring us peace."

Mr. Truman's efforts to get religious leaders to unite in an affirmation of faith dates to Myron C. Taylor's tenure as presidential envoy to the Vatican. Taylor first represented the late President Roosevelt and later Mr. Truman. He resigned in January, 1950 and has not been replaced. Protestant leaders have urged Mr. Truman to leave the post vacant.

On instructions from Mr. Truman, Taylor consulted with

church leaders in England, Germany, France, Switzerland, Greece and Turkey, as well as the Vatican.

In recent years the President himself has discussed his idea with church leaders in this country.

His statement tonight was the first time he has publicly expressed disappointment that his proposal has not borne fruit.

That Harry Truman should say in his appeal to Church leaders in 1951 that it was his idea to get the leaders of religion to cooperate, is not true as this book proves, but while I know the idea is not mine but that of our Lord the Christ and those Others who guide humanity, I give credit to Dean Acheson for appreciating its value and helping me to meet the top religious leaders. He accepted Justice Frankfurter's evaluation of this idea and after I had done the preliminary work, Acheson followed it up through Myron Taylor, but not to the Moslems nor to Indians, according to Truman. I had sent the following letters to Secretary of State Dean Acheson but no notice was taken of them, yet Islam, fanatically religious, is the most important ally the religious world could have against atheistic Communism. This the Catholic Church finally realized though no move was made by the Pope till 1952, 6 years after my appeal to him. But I had appealed after 1946 to others of the Roman Catholic clergy and my meeting with Sheikh Mustafa Abd-el Razek Pasha in 1946 had appeared on the front page of the *Boston Globe*, where at least the Massachusetts clergy of the Roman Catholic Church could read of the Sheikh's response and advice to me. I had kept Father John LaFarge informed of my moves and his voice would be listened to in Rome.

I give credit to Harry Truman in so far as he followed his Secretary of State's advice and I cannot but believe that his speech to the Christian religious leaders was probably written by Dean Acheson who wrote Truman's inaugural speech.

ALLIANCE WITH ISLAM?

Overshadowing all this, is the Pope's great design. This is to bring about a rapprochement between the Catholic church and Islam—without, of course, any compromise of religious dogma. Conversations have been encouraging. Spanish Foreign Minister Artajo's recent trip was fundamentally along these lines.

Commentators seemed to have overlooked the fact that Artajo is also the Secretary-General of Catholic Action in Spain.

The Pope's idea is a defensive alliance. He feels that stupendous and decisive events will take place in the Near and Middle East, and that only the closest accord between the Christian world and Islam can prevent Communism from establishing itself in this most important of all strategic areas.

The Intelligence Digest, London
July 1952

Dr. Franklin Fry in December 1949 was presiding at the Lutheran headquarters on Madison Avenue, formerly J. P. Morgan's town house. I went to him because he was on the Executive Council of the World Council of Churches and I hoped he would bring the idea of world prayer and cooperation to the members of the World Council. He did so but Dr. Henry Smith Leiper's letter explains that such suggestions must come from the church of the membership rather than from an individual. How the idea moves is not important to me, nor who suggests it providing it move. I am convinced this work has the blessing of our Lord and of all those whether in the flesh or in the Spirit who work for the love of the Almighty Spirit, that Spirit's will for the evolution of man and all creatures. Amen.

CHAPTER 8

LETTERS

THE FOLLOWING letters will be significant in showing the progress of the idea of my mission for Unity of the Spirit among men in high place in the religious life of America.

National Council of Negro Women, Inc.
1318 Vermont Avenue, Northwest
Washington 5, D. C.

January 2, 1948

TO WHOM IT MAY CONCERN

I am very happy to state that I know most interestingly, Comtesse Pierrefeu, and I am deeply interested in the fine work of spiritual unity and cooperation that she is extending to all races and nations throughout the world.

I think to have a chance to have her talk with any group, small or large, would be most beneficial to the group. Please know that I shall greatly appreciate your giving to her all cooperation possible in securing for her contact with people.

You will find her unbiased in her attitude toward mankind, deeply spiritual and unusually interested in the united power of those of us who have spiritual influence.

I am glad to call her "friend."

Sincerely yours,
Mary McLeod Bethune

ANDOVER-HARVARD THEOLOGICAL LIBRARY
Francis Avenue
Cambridge 38, Massachusetts

You will be interested to note that Chapter 19 in a new book, World Religions and the Hope for Peace by David Rhys Williams (Boston, Beacon Press, 1951) is on "The Golden Rule in all Religions."

Very sincerely

Nov. 25, 1951   Henry J. Cadbury

THE CHRISTIAN SCIENCE MONITOR
Published by The Christian Science Publishing Society
One, Norway Street, Boston 15, Massachusetts

October 14, 1948

Dear Comtesse de Pierrefeu:

Thank you for sending me your most inspiring compilation of the Golden Rule from various religions, and also your analysis of the great two Commandments.

I was most interested in the account in your letter of your efforts to bring together leadership in various religions. May you have all success in this noble effort.

Yours sincerely,
Erwin D. Canham
Editor

In 1946 in Paris I told my friend Marcelle Capy about the need for Unity in the Spirit. She had been through the German occupation and had been approached by the Communists as she was known for her brilliant public speaking, her novels, and the love and respect the working people had for her. She had seen the Communist power and knew their determination and materialism so she naturally refused. She was carried away by the idea I was working on and promised to help. The following alliance was the result.

L'ALLIANCE DES CROYANTS
pour l'Unité du Monde

Nous entrons dans l'ère atomique. Ce sera l'ère de l'unification du monde.

Ou cette unification sera seulement mécanique, et les hommes tomberont à l'état de matériel sous la loi implacable de la matière inanimée, après des convulsions cruelles et épuisantes;

ou les hommes retrouveront la raison et le sens de l'universel, et dirigeront l'outil du progrès matériel vers une unification vivante et amicale, liant la partie au tout et vice versa.

La politique et l'économie sont des aspects relatifs de la vie. Elles divisent et opposent les individus et les peuples. Leur impuissance a engendré le chaos.

On ne pourra s'en sortir et se sauver d'une déshumanisation générale et avilissante que par une vaste renaissance spirituelle et morale.

Il faut lever les yeux vers l'Absolu Idéal pour faire le point et naviguer juste sur l'océan des choses et des êtres.

D'abord, l'esprit. Le reste suit.

C'est à une œuvre de re-spiritualisation que se voue *l'Alliance des Croyants* qui naît sous le signe de l'amour des hommes pour l'amour de Dieu, et appelle tous ceux qui ont conscience de l'unité de la vie et du danger mortel qui menace l'humanité.

Quel que soit le nom par lequel ils désignent le Principe Suprême de l'univers, tous les spiritualistes fervents doivent aujourd'hui témoigner de la foi qui les anime, et se rapprocher afin de travailler au réveil des âmes et à la résurrection des valeurs sacrées communes à toutes les créatures humaines.

Toutes les grandes traditions religieuses et idéalistes ont proclamé et vénéré la Source Essentielle, éternelle, infinie et parfaite des mondes visibles et invisibles, et la communauté du destin humain.

C'est pourquoi, tous les Croyants peuvent et doivent faire alliance, à cette heure cruciale de l'évolution, pour élever les hommes à la conscience de leur responsabilité, de leur dignité, et de la fraternité exacte hors de laquelle il n'est point de salut.

La science et ses applications techniques ont donné à l'humanité un corps immense—, magnifique et redoutable à la fois, —qui se développe avec une implacable rigueur prenant les dimensions de la Terre.

Ce corps exige une âme à sa mesure. Il appartient aux Croyants de partout de donner l'impulsion nécessaire pour que cette âme soit.

Le temps de la vie isolée et dispersée s'achève.

Celui de l'unité commence.

Servons cette naissance. Et dépassons nos limitations passagères pour créer un climat spirituel de justice et d'amour sans lequel aucun des problèmes posés par la force des choses ne se pourra résoudre que dans l'esclavage et la mort.

Gardons chacun nos traditions comme chacun a sa famille.

Mais dressons au-dessus la grande famille des enfants de Dieu, ouverte à tous ceux, sans distinction, qui voient que l'heure est venue d'accomplir ce que les siècles ont préparé et dont nous avons maintenant les moyens: l'unité du monde par la fraternité des hommes, sous la souveraineté de l'Esprit.

Née de notre inébranlable foi, *l'Alliance des Croyants* s'agrandira de la vôtre.

Nous servirons ensemble l'Espérance et l'Amour universel.

Le Ciel nous aidera!

Marcelle CAPY.
Edouard SABY.

Adresser toute la correspondance aux promoteurs de l'Œuvre Marcelle CAPY et Edouard SABY, 10, rue Henri Duchène, Paris (XVe).

Translation of Madame Marcelle Capy's letter

Paris, Nov. 18, 1946

My dear Elsa;

We are trying with several friends to imitate your example and to create a women's group, a spiritual group uniting women who believe in the Spirit no matter what may be their religious belief or their philosophy. We have named this group, "The Spiritual Union of Women for Peace and Moral Renewal." I hope that we shall succeed with the help of the Holy Spirit that we wish to serve and in spite of present circumstances which make life so hard. We have asked Catholics, Protestants, Jews, Theosophists, Spiritualists in the large sense of the word. If we succeed in forming this group, this center of spirituality, we must then do our best to keep it shining in spite of the dark clouds of materialism that surround us.

Let us follow in the footsteps of St. Francis of Assisi;

Dear Lord, may I be an instrument of your peace;
"Where there is hatred, may I bring love;
"Where there is offense, may I pardon;
"Where there is discord, may I bring peace;
"Where there is error, may I bring truth;
"Where there is doubt, may I bring faith;
"Where there is despair, may I bring hope;
"Where there is darkness, may I bring light;
"Where there is sorrow, may I bring joy.
"Dear Lord, may I not seek consolation but to console;
"To be understood, but to understand,
"To be loved but to love, because it is by giving oneself that we receive, by forgetting oneself that we find ourselves, by forgiving that we are forgiven, it is by dying that we rise again to eternal life."

May God bless you very dear Elsa, I embrace you with all my heart,

Marcelle.

THE FEDERAL COUNCIL
OF THE
CHURCHES OF CHRIST IN AMERICA
Office of the General Secretary
297 Fourth Avenue
New York

October 4, 1943

Dear Countess:

I have been interested to learn of your plan for a world-wide day of prayer. Your conception is a noble one. You doubtless realize how great the difficulties are in securing a concert of prayer which will be really worldwide, but I hope that you may be successful. We shall all be greatly pleased if you can realize your dream.

Cordially yours,
Samuel McCrea Cavert
General Secretary

UNITED NATIONS—NATIONS UNIES
LAKE SUCCESS, NEW YORK

9 June 1949

Dear Mr. Leiper,

Many thanks for your letter of 2 June addressed to the Secretary-General. Mme. de Pierrefeu's suggestions has been used in lectures about the United Nations and will also be followed in some adequate radio programs.

Sincerely yours,
B. Cohen
Assistant Secretary-General
for Public Information

ALDERBOURNE MANOR,
GERRARDS CROSS,
BUCKINGHAMSHIRE.

26th June, 1952.

Dear Madame de Pierrefeu,

Very many thanks for your most interesting letter of the 14th June.

I am so glad that you feel as we do the necessity for a great spiritual awakening. A significant fact may interest you, and that is that about two years ago we had many letters complaining of the inclusion of spiritual matters in "Intelligence Digest." These have now ceased completely, and we have as many letters now wholeheartedly agreeing with us.

With renewed thanks,

Intelligence Digest

Yours sincerely,
Kenneth de Courcy.

GENERAL FEDERATION OF WOMEN'S CLUBS

1944-1947
President
Mrs. LaFell Dickinson

February 15, 1945.

Dear Madame de Pierrefeu:

I am very sure that when the time comes to have the Day of Prayer for the whole world that the General Federation of Women's Clubs will do all it can to promote it.

Certainly no matter what our belief is, we should be able to take one day to ask that God make us worthy of living in this world. I think it is marvelous that you are giving all your time to this.

It was nice to see you in Keene, and when the appropriate time comes, we shall be glad to help if we can.

Very Sincerely yours,
Lucy J. Dickinson
Mrs. LaFell Dickinson
President

152

THE UNION OF AMERICAN HEBREW
CONGREGATIONS
Cincinnati, Ohio

September 12, 1944

Dear Madame de Pierrefeu:

I was very much interested in your recent letter concerning your plan for instituting a day of peace and prayer for all religions. I agree with you thoroughly that there is certainly need of spiritual unity between man and man, and I am happy to add my hearty approval and endorsement of your plan. I also want you to know that you can count upon my full co-operation in this fine undertaking.

Yours most sincerely,
Maurice N. Eisendrath
Director

SUPREME COURT OF THE UNITED STATES
Washington, D. C.

Chambers of
JUSTICE FELIX FRANKFURTER

March 16, 1945

My dear Madame de Pierrefeu:

Your general aim is so humane, however difficult its achievement, that I cannot help but have a sense of guilt not to be able to further it. But as I tried to indicate to you when you were here, the judicial office is the most circumscribing of any. While I am in the world I am largely not of it, and certainly not in any aspects that others, if not you, would recognize as political.

Sincerely yours,
Felix Frankfurter

Dear Sister, I would gladly co-
operate. But in the midst
of my poverty I doubt the utility
of our posite public fast,
fasting & prayer of the type
you have in mind sho'ld be in
secret and with a definite
object.
                    Yours sin...ly
                    mkgandhi

UNION THEOLOGICAL SEMINARY

Committee on Graduate Study

New York, January 19, 1950

My dear Comtesse:

Thank you for your letter of January 17th. I am heartily in sympathy with a proposal to invite all mankind to pray for peace, and I am especially glad to hear that Mr. l'Heureux has interested the veterans' organizations and others in such a prayer. Under separate cover I am sending you a copy of one of our weekly church papers—*The Witness* for January 19th. You will be interested in the editorial.

Sincerely yours,
Frederick C. Grant

606 West 122nd Street
New York City

5 February, 1955

Dear Countess de Pierrefeu:

I do not remember my letter of 1950, but I am still in favor of prayers for peace—prayers by everyone, if possible. To say the very least, if the great majority of mankind were praying for peace, they could not at the same time be engaged in killing one another. Except that man is a very stupid creature, in some ways, and does not recognize his own inconsistency.

With every good wish,

Sincerely yours,
Frederick C. Grant

Lynsted, 25 St. Edmund's Terrace, Regent's Park, N. W.

25th October, 1948

My dear Countess Tudor de Pierrefeu,

Thank you so much for your most kind letter and excellent Golden Rules. Indeed, as Sheik Abd-el-Razek told you, it is the spiritual food for which the earth is starving. I am sure he continues to help you from the other side.

Many thanks too for sending me your *National Anti-Vivesection Magazine*.

Yours affectionately,
Nina Hamilton
(Duchess of Hamilton
and Brandon)

WORLD WIDE BROADCASTING FOUNDATION
WRUL
133 Commonwealth Avenue
Boston 16, Massachusetts

November 8, 1949

Dear Comtesse:

Thank you for your letter of October 31.

Our minds must have been in tune, because on October 30

and subsequent Sundays I made use of the material which you left with me.

Our program time on Sundays is somewhat limited by the fact that all of the programs are on records, but I included the following quotation in our announcements:

"The whole length and breadth of the world is pervaded by the radiant thoughts of a mind all-embracing, vast and boundless, in which dwells no hate nor ill will. That is a Buddhist concept of God. The Confucianist says that all things originate in and from Heaven. The Hindus—He is the Creator, He is the Disposer. He himself is one, single, one only. The Islamic believer states: He is the First and the Last, the Seen and the Hidden. And we, as Christians, recognize our common relationship with these, our brothers, saying: There is but one God, The Father, of whom are all things, and we in Him."

Thank you very much for giving me this material, and I hope that you will come in again when you are in Boston.

Sincerely yours,
Wyman Holmes (Signed)
Boston Manager.

July 21, 1941

My dear Comtesse:

I am sympathetic to your "day of prayer" idea. The Synagogue Council will not meet again until September. Is this too late for your plans? I think, however, I can give you the assurance that *if* the Catholics and Protestants are ready to go ahead, and *if* the public announcement will be on a strictly *interfaith*, interdenominational basis, I can speak for the Synagogue Council in advance.

At present I am summering for a few weeks in Maine. My address is Bangor, Me., R.F.D. #1, % Gould's Landing.

Let me know how things develop. I shall co-operate fully.

Sincerely,
Edward L. Israel

RUFUS M. JONES
Haverford College
Haverford, Pa.

3-29-1944

Dear friend,

Many thanks for your interesting letter of the 22nd. I am sending you a copy of our letter to persons who may wish to join the Wider Quaker Fellowship and I hope this may be a preliminary to eventually joining the Society of Friends when the time comes for it.

I should hardly think it wise to go forward with your plan for a day of fasting and prayer for all religions unless you can get the support of the major leaders of religious life and thought in different parts of the world. But you are a better judge of the amount of support you have already received than I can be.

Very sincerely your friend,
Rufus M. Jones

150 Fifth Avenue, New York City

August 6, 1941

My dear Comtesse:

Thank you so much for your letter, which I have read with great interest. I fully approve of these different faiths coming together for a day of prayer, and I will be glad to do all I can in regard to it. We are having an all-night vigil for prayer tonight, that our country may be guided of God.

With my best wishes for you and your work,

Yours very sincerely,
E. Stanley Jones

AMERICA
National Catholic Weekly Review

New York, January 26, 1955

Dear Comtesse de Pierrefeu:

Surely you can quote me as saying: "Comtesse de Pierrefeu's story of her heroic pilgrimage in quest of a world crusade of prayer is inspiring and it is a testimony to her own faith in God and man. It is a message much needed in the present day."

Best wishes from

Sincerely yours,
Rev. John LaFarge, S.J.

EPISCOPAL PACIFIST FELLOWSHIP
Affiliated with the Fellowship of Reconciliation

January 9, 1942

My dear Madame de Pierrefeu:

Thank you for your letter with its enclosures. Yes, I had heard of the Universal Christian Council's request to pray at 6:00 p.m.

You have indeed had an interesting correspondence with various persons all over the world, and I certainly congratulate you on the results, which I shall be glad to bring before the next meeting of the E.P.F. Executive Committee, scheduled for the thirteenth of this month.

I had not heard of the incident when your mother and my father fell into Jamaica Pond. That is a new one on me.

Yours gratefully,
(Bishop) W. Appleton Lawrence

DIOCESE OF WESTERN MASSACHUSETTS
Office of the Bishop
Springfield, 5, Massachusetts
37 Chestnut Street
The Rt. Rev. W. Appleton Lawrence, D. D.
Bishop

February 29, 1944

My dear Comtesse:

I guess that as long as the war is on, your way to India will be blocked, and I do not believe that anything Bishop Tucker could say would make any difference, even if he wanted to say it.

It is true, of course, that our ties with the Anglican Church restrict our labors in some ways, but in other ways we are strengthened by the association. Also, for better or for worse, I guess we will have to face facts.

As to your ideas on conscription. If the conscription were for non-military purposes, I would feel there was some sense in it, but I do not see how the two can be combined. As a matter of fact, I am not over-hopeful that our protest will be much more than a gesture, but I do think we ought to make it, nonetheless.

Yours faithfully,
W. Appleton Lawrence

THE UNIVERSAL CHRISTIAN COUNCIL
FEDERAL COUNCIL OF THE CHURCHES
OF CHRIST IN AMERICA

New York, June 5, 1935

My dear Mrs. Tudor:

Since we talked together I have had other bulletins from Europe, and letters showing that the project for concerted prayer is really being seriously followed by the leaders of many great communions. I had one note from the Procurator of the Holy Synod of the Greek Orthodox Church, and another from the Secretary of the National Christian Council of Japan. Every effort will be made to keep the matter before those who can make it effective on the widest possible scale.

With good wishes for the summer months and your own activities, which I know are not interrupted by the vacation season, I am

> Faithfully yours,
> Henry Smith Leiper,
> Executive Secretary

THE UNIVERSAL CHRISTIAN COUNCIL
287 Fourth Avenue, New York City

December 16, 1941

My dear Mrs. de Pierrefeu:

You will be interested to know that it has now been definitely decided to call for a moment of prayer every day at six o'clock in this country, and that this is being done quite widely in other lands. It is not quite the same idea as the one which you have discussed of a day, but perhaps it will accomplish something of the same purpose, and I knew that you would like to know about it.

Thanking you for your interest and your deep devotion to the cause of a happier and better world, I am,

> Yours faithfully,
> Henry Smith Leiper

HENRY SMITH LEIPER
297 Fourth Avenue
New York City

January 8, 1946

My dear Mr. Byrnes:

I understand that Madame Alain de Pierrefeu, of Hancock, New Hampshire, who has for many years been interested in various useful projects dedicated to international understanding, is contemplating a trip to Europe, Egypt, and possibly to India.

I should like to associate myself with Dr. Rufus Jones, Mr. Henry Cadbury, and Archbishop Cushing, of the Roman Catholic Church, in supporting her request for the aid of the Department in her mission which, I am sure, can only help a cause in which we all have a deep interest.

Yours faithfully,
Henry Smith Leiper

The Hon. James Francis Byrnes
Department of State
Washington, D. C.

G. BROMLEY OXNAM
Bishop of The Methodist Church
100 Maryland Avenue, N. E., Washington 2, D. C.

December 13, 1954

My dear Comtesse:

I sincerely trust that you will forgive what must appear to you to be an inexcusable discourtesy. Your lovely letter of September 8 reached me immediately following the Second Assembly of the World Council of Churches which was held in Evanston, Illinois. I set it aside to answer as soon as I had caught up with the very heavy correspondence that was awaiting me upon my return from that Assembly. I do not understand how it could have been misplaced, but it was, and it has only now come to my attention as I have gone through some files covering items that I thought had been cared for.

In an hour when the spiritual view of life is challenged as perhaps at no time in history, it is imperative that all who believe there is a Father of us all should join hands, or better, should fall upon our knees together, first in worship, and then in confession of our own sins, and finally in a petition for the power that is essential for us to rise and go out and build a better world. There is much being done toward this end, as you know, although limited outlook, intolerance, and bigotry at times make it difficult for us to work together. This is unforgivable. I am sure that what you are seeking to do must commend itself to all thinking and devoted people.

Once again, pardon the long delay in answering your important letter.

Ever sincerely yours,
G. Bromley Oxnam

Clarence E. Pickett
20 South 12th Street
Philadelphia 7, Penna.

January 15, 1947

Dear Friend:

I have received your letter telling of your visits to England, France, Italy, Egypt, etc. I was particularly glad that you had a chance to visit with Lady Parmoor whom I know well, together with her sister, Edith Ellis. They are very dear friends of ours.

Whether the proposed plan for cooperation around the world in fasting and prayer can take place or not, I think your visits to these persons may be of value. I hope that you may find divine guidance in your entire experience and I shall be glad to hear from you further when you get back.

Sincerely yours,
Clarence E. Pickett

Bishop Reverdy C. Ransom
Tawawa Chimney Corner
Wilberforce, Ohio

March 12, 1945

Dear Madam:

Your letter to me under date of March 4 reads like an answer to prayer. The attitude and the objectives held and cherished by you are among the things I have labored, hoped, and prayed for many years to see realized. Be assured I shall be pleased to cordially cooperate with the objectives set forth in your letter to me. Many of the signers are personally known to me.

I think our American ideals are the highest and best set forth by any nation in the world because underneath they are based upon the teachings of Jesus. As nations go, we are a young nation, which in the past, has made substantial progress and is now, I believe, through spirits like yours, girding itself to make larger strides toward the goal of cordial relations among people of different creeds, colors, and national derivation who compose the many different varieties of the human race. If American democracy and American christianity cannot achieve complete freedom of opportunity economically, socially, and politically for all, then our hopes, our prayers, and our strivings shall seem to be in vain.

Your allusion to Thomas Wentworth Higginson strikes a tender note within me when I recall how many noble spirits like him and Robert Gould Shaw staked all they had to Preserve the Union and Establish Freedom within our borders. It is good to know there are people like you alive and active in our midst. Since the world is now rapidly becoming one great neighborhood, the men and women of good will throughout all nations should unite and use the weight of their influence for the realization of the world's long cherished dream of peace, justice, brotherhood.

Faithfully yours,
Reverdy C. Ransom

PROTESTANT EPISCOPAL CHURCH
In the United States of America
Office of the Presiding Bishop
281 Fourth Avenue
New York 10, N. Y.
The Rt. Rev. Henry K. Sherrill, D.D.

March 10, 1955

Dear Madame de Pierrefeu,

It is with great interest I have read the manuscript of your book. Certainly it is most impressive to realize the years you have given to a most worthwhile project, namely bringing about a better understanding between men of various nations, races and religions, based upon spiritual understanding and prayer.

I found the story of your work most interesting.

Faithfully yours,
Henry K. Sherrill
PRESIDING BISHOP

THE CARAVAN OF EAST AND WEST, INC.
132 East 65th Street
New York 21, N. Y., U. S. A.

October 5, 1949

Countess A. de Pierrefeu
Dear Champion of World Relations:

I read your letter dated third instant enclosing a printed leaflet of the golden rules of the great religions of the world. I think that you have rendered a great service to the cause of brotherhood in bringing to the attention of the U.N. and broadcasting stations this supreme question for the unity and identity of the fundamentals of all religions.

M. A. Sohrab
(Director)
(An offshoot of Bahai-Teaching)

164

HARVARD DIVINITY SCHOOL
Andover Hall, Francis Avenue
Cambridge, Massachusetts

Office of the Dean September 21, 1943

Dear Countess de Pierrefeu:

Please forgive my delay in sending you this promised letter. As you saw, I was—and still am—housed, and have to get on with my correspondence slowly.

You laid before me your hope that, somehow or other, a world-wide day of fasting and prayer might be arranged in which all religious folk of good will might feel united in what would be a common act of penitence and self-dedication.

No one who cares for religion can for a moment question the desirability of such a day and such an act, and many individuals and religious bodies would be glad to be identified with such an act and associated together in its observance. The principle is simple and clear; there remains the matter of practice.

As you well enough know, no single individual or small group of individuals can hope to promote the organization necessary for the effective observance of such a day. It would have to be done through existing religious bodies.

If it is done, it should be done freely and *con amore*, as a co-operative act, so that each participating body recognizes to the full the right of others to share in the act. If I were you I should stress this latter point in whatever further approaches you make.

With best wishes,

Sincerely yours,
W. H. Sperry

HARVARD DIVINITY SCHOOL
Andover Hall, Francis Avenue
Cambridge, Massachusetts

Office of the Dean   November 18, 1943

My dear Comtesse:

I am glad that you have made such headway with your project. You have vision and good courage, and what is known in New England as "stick-to-itiveness." Apparently my suggestion that you should see some of the heads of church organizations in the country has not been unprofitable.

I am interested that you saw Stanley Hornbeck. He is a personal friend of mine and, of course, knows a great deal about the Far East.

I will see that a letter is put in Bishop Tucker's hands to become part of the material to be presented to the President in behalf of your hoped-for visit to India.

Certainly events are moving very rapidly, and the sooner right-minded people can get ahead with any and all plans for spiritual unity throughout the world, the better for the post-war world.

With all good wishes,

Sincerely yours,
W. H. Sperry

11 Francis Avenue
Cambridge 38, Massachusetts

Jan. 19, 1946

Dear Madame de Pierrefeu,

You have been very fortunate to get the way cleared for your proposed visit to Europe, Egypt and India.

Your mission is in service of the most imperative of all causes and prompted by the highest motives.

And I congratulate you on the "nameless friend" who got

you access to the State Department. As I told you, we here in the University are unable to make such appeals.

I do wish you well on your "pilgrimage of faith," for it is such.

Sincerely yours,
W. H. Sperry

MARY E. WOOLLEY
"Fleur De Lys"
Westport, Essex County
New York

March 22, 1944

My dear Friend:

Your letter of the sixteenth I have read several times,—I am sure that you know with what sympathy and understanding. I think you are right in feeling that you must keep your thought alive "until men everywhere want to unite in Spirit." I am not a pessimist and I have little sympathy with those who feel that human nature is human nature and there is no hope of progress in this great question of human relationships. On the other hand, although it is hard to be patient, I think I realize increasingly that the change in human attitudes and understanding will come slowly.

Indeed, I am "willing to go as far as Bishop Tucker and Father LaFarge and Swami Premananda." Bishop Tucker exactly expresses my point of view and I am more than glad to "follow after."

Does the above answer your question?

Affectionately yours,
Mary E. Woolley

(Former President of Mt. Holyoke College; Delegate from the United States to the League of Nations.)